The Four Questions Of Life

Brian Gray

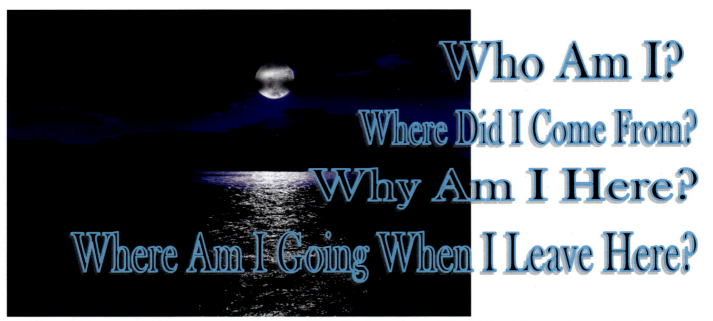

There they are, the four questions that haunt us all of our lives. We think of them subconsciously for a long time, but there comes a day when we start to think of them consciously. We start asking. Who am I? Really? Who am I? Oh sure, I am the child of my parents, the grandchild of my proud grandparents, I can trace my lineage, but there comes a time in everyone's life when we begin to feel like there is something more to our unique and very personal identity. Like the stars in the sky, we sense our individuality.

And where did I come from? Beyond my parents, did I exist before I came here? What is my purpose for being here? Was I supposed to become someone famous and great? Was I supposed to be very wealthy? Have I failed that destiny? Why am I here, now, in this time on Earth of all the times into which I could have been born? And when I die, where am I going? Is there a Hell? Is there a Heaven? Or is there someplace else that they are just not telling us about? Where am I going when I leave this plane of existence?

The more intelligent you are, the more you think. You are taught your beliefs from childhood. Parents, older relatives, school teachers, religious leaders, friends, the list goes on and on of all the people who influence your ideas of what is right and wrong, how to act, even what to wear. There are so many "molding" influences in your life, that it is hard to separate them from who the real "you" is. Add to that list where you were born, in what century, what ethnicity, and the "molding" becomes even more influential. Are you Chinese, or are you French? Do you live on a farm, or do you live in a city? Are you a Christian, or are you Jewish? Do your parents have college educations, or are you from a broken home with one parent who dropped out of school? These influences are just the beginning, and we all get constantly bombarded and confused in that forest. Become molded into the image others make for you, or break free and create your own identity; some find their way out, while others perish in the maze of life's conforming pressures.

Every religion that has ever been invented has an ending for you that is dependent on whether you have been good or bad during your lifetime as judged by fellow human beings beset with the same frailties and foibles as you. I am here to show you the truth about the answers to the four questions of life.

Brian Gray

October 11, 2020

What is Sin?

    I heard the loud sound of someone huffing and puffing with obvious difficulty in their struggle, and I turned to behold an old man with a huge bundled sack on his shoulders. The sight of someone so worn out from what immediately appeared to have been a very hard life, and to be showing all the signs of such travails, vexed me greatly. Bent nearly double with the weight, the gnarled relic of a human being was half the size of his heavy load. Greatly perplexed, I wondered aloud as to why he was carrying so great a burden.

    "Why, I must!" he replied with near indignant astonishment at my question. "I must, I must, I must... until I die, I must carry these, or I shall lose my reward," he intoned methodically, as if singing a religious hymn.

    "What reward?" I inquired with genuine intrigue.

    As if I had asked a silly question, and without shifting even so much as one ounce of the burdensome weight to the ground for relief, the withered old man replied,

    "Why, when I reach my goal, I will be rewarded for having carried all of these faithfully to the very end of my course. It's a great reward," he added reassuringly.

    "Can you describe this reward?" I asked.

    "Well, it's a better house in a better city," he replied.

    "And have you seen this house?" I pondered further.

    "No, but I have heard many people talk about it, and they say it is wonderful," he responded with a nearly blissful smile.

"And what is in this great bag which you carry?" I inquired.

"Why, they are lists of restrictions... many, many, many restrictions," he answered with utmost seriousness.

"Restrictions?" I mused, "What on earth do you mean?"

"Well," he began, "I am not sure about some of them, because I have never had the time to study all of them..."

His voice seemed to trail for a moment, pensive, then he picked back up with some fervor,

"... but they are for my benefit, and if I carry all of these to the end of my journey, then I receive my reward."

"And who gave you these 'restrictions'?" I asked with even more intrigue.

"Well," he began, "I have never met him, because he died many years ago, but we follow his directions, because we know he knew more than we do... and we all want that reward, you know," said the old man with a strange joy. And with that, he said,

"Well, I must be off, got a ways to go yet, and

someone told me that there were some more restrictions waiting for me just ahead. I look forward to putting those in my bag. That should really add to my house in that city."

I watched with great puzzlement as the old man struggled to keep the load from falling and slowly shuffled out of sight. A great burden handed to him by others, messages of restrictions written by someone other than himself, many unread and mysterious as to their logic, but he carried all of them on his back with pride, all because of the great reward he had been told would be his for this arduous task... a reward he had to accept by faith... for the load he had to accept by fact.

And it becomes obvious to most who read this far that the symbolism here employed is the definition of "sin." "Sin" is any one of a list of religious restrictions thought up by others than ourselves and then forced on others who blindly follow without question. A method used to keep children in line is to tell them what is defined as "wrongdoing" and what the consequences are of committing that "wrongdoing." Misbehaving equates with punishment that is given once the parents find out about those infractions. Funny how we grow into adults and use the same equation for religious teachings. We are taught that God is our Father, and if we commit "sin," God will be displeased and will even punish us. At some point, the person telling us that God is not pleased by "sin" will give us a list of what things constitute "sin." And, because we don't want to lose out with God, we follow whatever that person lists as the great "Do Nots."

I was raised in the Fundamentalist sect of Christianity, and I remember once, as a child, being severely frustrated that everything my schoolmates were allowed to go and do for fun was off limits to me. I couldn't do this, and I couldn't do that, and it all boiled over one day as I whined to my father, who was a preacher,

"Daddy, our religion is just a bunch of don'ts. We can't do ANYTHING!" My father was taken aback by that comment and told me that such was not true, but his comment to the contrary did not change my view at the time. I could not go to the movies, I could not go bowling, I could not play any games that involved dice, I could not go to the beach, I could not wear shorts in public in the summer time, I could not listen to "worldly music" (I had my secret stash of Motown records), I could not dance, I could not wear any jewelry, I could not wear stylish clothes... and the list went on and on. Yes, my religion was a religion of "don'ts." And where did these "don'ts" come from? Well, they sure didn't come from me! I remember that, by the time I had gotten to college, the words of Jesus weighed heavily on me regarding the subject of religious restrictions. In Matthew 11:30, Jesus said that His yoke was easy and His burden was light, so why did I feel so constrained and burdened by the religious restrictions that I followed like a fanatic zealot? I was carrying a huge bag of restrictions, and virtually all of them had been placed in my bag by others.

By the time I was in college, I had become a fanatical religious zealot, striving to become a modern-day Apostle Paul for all of my strict religious observances. In later years, I would come to discover that "religious" is not necessarily "spiritual," and as someone once wisely observed, **"A religious man follows the dictates of his church; a spiritual man follows the dictates of his soul."** I had to learn the difference. Let me say right here that we can all create a list of "sins," but they are founded on human frailty, human desire to be closer to God, and while personal sacrifice may yield a style of living that is productive for each of us individually, your personal list of restrictions has absolutely nothing to do with mine. If you invent a list, "you" invented that list. Follow it if you choose, for good or for worse, but to inflict that on others truly fulfills the old saying that misery loves company.

Martin Luther was on his way to becoming a prominent lawyer in Germany when he was caught in a terrible storm, and fearing for his life, he prayed to Saint Anne, the patroness saint of miners, and promised that, if she would save him from this terrible storm, he would become a monk. When the storm suddenly abated, Martin Luther kept his unwarranted promise and entered a monastery. One of his experiences has always stuck with me. He determined that, in his bid to become closer to God, he should not sleep with comfortable blankets. So, Martin Luther replaced his blankets with rough burlap. Eventually, he felt that his bed, likewise, was "sinfully" comfortable and did not provide the spiritual sacrifice needed to get closer to God, so he began to sleep on the stone floor. Eventually, he got rid of the pillow, and eventually, even the burlap blanket, reasoning that being warm was an indulgence that he should forgo. And there lay Martin Luther on that cold, stone floor thinking to himself that, after all of this constant self-sacrifice, he was still no closer to God. He could kill himself with self-deprivations, and he would still be no closer to God. Eventually, Martin Luther left the monastery and applied reasoning to his pursuit of religious beliefs. Is sleeping on a bed with warm blankets a sin? There would be a time when Martin Luther might have not only felt that the answer was in the affirmative, but had he not had the legal mind that he did, he may have added some new sins to someone else's list. Later, Martin Luther studied the words of the Apostle Paul, wherein he said, "The just shall live by faith," and this opened his mind to understanding that there is nothing we can do as physical action to earn closeness to God. **Our faith in God is sufficient to inherit that position.**

One of the tenets of Christianity is that the crucifixion of Jesus Christ did away with the rituals of animal sacrifices that were so common, and made it so that all who became believers would no longer have to observe the established lists of sins and their requisite sacrifices. Still, there are many who follow Christianity and who, while not sacrificing animals on an altar, regularly have their own versions of sacrifice for sins on a list that they have created for themselves, lists that were actually authored and handed to them by others.

What is sin? And, who determines the answer to that question? These are two very important questions, because, like the old man I described in the beginning of this discussion, **if we do not know what the word actually means, we can become weighted down with a collection of edicts formulated by others who are as unqualified to answer that question as they are to place those unnecessary burdens on us.** Studying the question of "sin," people will ask me, what is "sin," and why do so many Christians teach their various "lists?" The word "sin" goes back through the centuries to the Old English noun, "synn," meaning "moral wrongdoing, injury, mischief, enmity, feud, guilt, crime, offense against God, misdeed," and this word goes further back to the Latin "sons/sont," meaning "guilty." Further back, still, we find that the Greeks had several words to define the various types of "sins" and their relative intensity, but the word used for what we translate as "sin" would be the Greek word ἁμαρτία, "hamartia," an archery term that simply means "to miss the mark." And this goes back to the ancient Hebrew word, חטא, "chata," which, once again, means "to miss the mark." What a person finds when reading the Bible, whether it is the Old or New Testament, is that the more religious people became, the more they expected that there

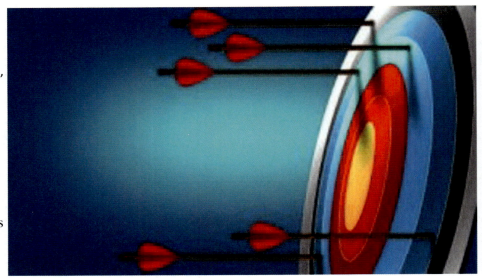

should be given them a list of restrictions that would keep them from incurring the wrath of God, as well as to ensure that they would live with God in the afterlife. Those "lists" have varied over the centuries, along with their human authors, and the description of the reward in the afterlife has equally varied. Even the "Seven Deadly Sins" is a list created by a human being, Pope Gregory I, to be exact, around the year A.D. 600. So, the question arises even more importantly, "What is sin?" Or, is there such a thing, then, as "sin?"

Humans have tried to make lists of sins ever since we first appeared on the planet. Lists, and punishments for violating those lists, read like bizarre documents from another planet. Though civilized countries have pretty much gotten away from mandating laws that punish citizens for religious sins, it has not been that long ago that we Westerners did, and we are still paying for the residual effect of having had the Church dictate civil law for so many centuries. Not too long ago, civilians could be put to death, and routinely were, for violating the lists of sins cranked out by the Church. When Spanish explorers conquered South American kingdoms, they were known to extort the conversion of the rulers to Christianity, then summarily execute them before they could lapse into a return to their cultural religions... saving souls from "backsliding." To see the barbarism and lack of spirituality in so many man-made religious edicts in this current day and age, one need only go to such third-world countries as Afghanistan or Pakistan, and one will see countless examples of women being stoned to death for such "sins" as being rape victims, or even for being "shamefully dressed," otherwise known as too short of a veil exposing hair on the head.

Have we Westerners been "weird" about sin? In 18th and 19th Century Europe, Christians observed the custom of "sin eating." If a person died, he or she might have some sins that were not confessed prior to death, so, a "sin eater" was hired. A slice of bread, or a vessel of wine or beer, would be placed on the body

An illustration by Francois Marie Balanant, born in France, August 24, 1737,

showing the heart and the Seven Deadly Sins

Clockwise, each sin is represented by an animal.:

Toad = Avarice; Snake = Envy; Lion = Wrath; Snail = Sloth; Pig = Gluttony; Goat = Lust; Peacock = Pride of the deceased. The sins went into the food, and the sin eater would then consume the bread or wine and thus consume the sins, leaving the deceased cleansed in the afterlife. Even today, joking phrases such as "living in sin," meaning living together without the blessings of a Church marriage ceremony, were once severely punished by laws that originated in the Church. And if you think for one minute that questioning the authority of the Church to enumerate a list of sins and relative punishments is out of the question, America was founded on a strong desire to be free of that very same powerful persecution. Colonial settlers knew all too well the effect on their lives when human beings became religious zealots, formed religious institutions, then gained the power to mandate public laws. The long road to freedom in the United States has been strengthened by the principle of Separation of Church and State.

I remember when I personally began to question "The List." I was sitting in church one Sunday, and a very beloved preacher was well into his sermon when he said the following: "Rock and Roll music will take your soul straight to Hell! But, now, Country music... well, that's God's music." He smiled benignly when he said "Country music," as if everyone in that congregation knew exactly what he meant and agreed wholeheartedly. Yep, they all liked Country music, and they all hated Rock and Roll, so... "Amen!" Rock and Roll music made it to the "The List." When I was a teenager, being caught listening to "worldly" music could result in punishment, so we would wait until our parents were out of the house to turn on the radio and listen to our favorites, all while one of us kept a lookout for the car arriving in the driveway. There was many a close call when I looked out the window to hear car doors closing and barely managed to get that LP off of the record player in time to flee to the bedroom and stash those "immoral" records in their hiding place.

In all seriousness, the Bible contains passages that rail against the various societal lapses of the day, from the prophets of ancient Israel to the apostles of the Early Church, but even these two groups would have disagreed on what was sin and what was not, such is "moral evolution." However, the principle remains, we do not want to "miss the mark." And there is a "mark" for which we should be aiming. What is that "mark?" **Destiny With Our Creator.** I have intentionally made that phrase all capitals for a reason, that being, you should stop and think about that phrase all throughout your life. Destiny? Destiny with what? **Destiny with Death, with the life beyond this plane of existence.** It is easy to get caught up with man-made "lists," lists that are for religious parrots who think and act like children, when the real focus should be on what happens when the adult in the room, "The Question Of Death," comes knocking at your door for a conversation. As the old Amish proverb says, "We grow too soon old and too late smart." So, why wait until death to start thinking seriously about the Four Questions of Life? And those four questions are: **Who am I? Where did I come from? Why am I here? Where am I going when I leave here?** Ignore them all you want to, but they WILL be answered... in due time, either here in this plane of existence, or on the other side of this plane.

The concept of Heaven and Hell has been an ever-evolving one, even in the Bible. Do good, you are rewarded, do bad, and you are punished, nothing new with that theme, and if you go to any church in America and engage in a conversation with the members, it does not take long before "The List" is trotted out, and you are told who is excluded from "Heaven." I remember many years ago listening to a sermon preached by an elder African-American preacher from Pittsburgh named Reverend E.D. Cobb, and I will never forget his opening line. He said, "Some of you, when you get to Heaven, you're going to look around and say, 'Well, look who's here!'" I believe, from my experience with an out-of-body event described later in this book, that there is indeed life after this one. I believe that some Creator Force has a purpose for my existence. It seems logical that this Creator Force has designed "Who am I? Where did I come from? Why am I here? and Where am I going when I leave here?" Strangely, the Bible gives us two clues as to the proper religious view regarding "sin." The Apostle Paul, while in a discussion about "sins," says in I Corinthians 10:23 that "**All things are lawful, but not all things are profitable.**" Think about that for a moment. All things are lawful. In other words, everything you do, regardless of religious prohibition, is not actually to be restricted by some religious edict, but, and here is the big "but" - not all things are profitable. If what you are doing will cause you to be unprepared for the transition at death, then what you are doing will cause you to "miss the mark," and is, therefore, "unprofitable." And in Micah 6:8, "**He hath shewed thee, O man, what is good; and what doth the LORD require of thee, but to do justly, to love mercy, and to walk humbly before your God?**" So, you have the lists of man, and you have the requirements of your Creator. One list seems to be a bit shorter than the other.

If we were to take all of the sin "Lists" that have been put together by human beings since time began, and we tried to live by them, we would look like religious pretzels with more convolutions than dried prunes. For each person, there are rules that help that person get through life, and these rules are not the same from person to person. We each do daily battle with "Self" and all its natural flaws and pitfalls. The path ahead is a forked road, and we each decide which path to take—one leading to happiness at death, the other leading to a fear of death. We either hit the mark and end this existence satisfied, or we end it regretful. While some would have us flagellating ourselves daily with whips, literally, I think God would have us live this life free from the Hell that zealots have created for us. Maybe that is one of the reasons He sent Jesus Christ to tell us that we are free from the label of "sinners," that with His sacrifice, and through the grace of that act, we are to accept, as Paul said, that all things are lawful, but not all things are profitable... in other words, don't allow yourself to be detoured, to be taken off of the path that leads to being spiritually satisfied when it comes your turn to leave this plane of existence. Aim properly, and you won't "miss the mark."

All religions have created their lists of "sins." One thing I mention often is that all adherents to all religions have one thing in common: they are all going to die. Regardless of the religion you choose, or the atheistic approach you otherwise follow, you will all go through the door of Death. As I will discuss throughout this book, there really IS something beyond this existence. How you prepare for it is colored by your religious upbringing, but your religious upbringing will not alter one thing, and that is the reality that is beyond this life. So, whether you are flagellating yourself with religious edicts, or a total hedonist who cares about nothing, the river of life flows onward toward your ultimate destiny. Maybe it is time you stopped for a moment and thought about what that is so that you can enjoy the comfort and peace that truly knowing the answer to the four questions of life will bring to you.

Who Am I?

 The first of the Four Questions: Who am I? Look around you. How many people look exactly like you? Even if you were born as a twin, your twin will not be an exact duplicate of you. When you scan the world around you, something is very apparent; you are not connected by some physical cord to anyone else. Yes, you are born into a family, and, as the old saying goes, "Blood is thicker than water," so, you are connected in many ways to your family, but this is not what I am referring to. The only thoughts that you can read are the ones in your head. What does that mean to you? Look at the person standing in front of you at any given time. There is a world inside their head, a world that you will never even come close to exploring or understanding, a world based on all of their experiences, and you can never tap into the completeness of it. There is a wall between your mental world, that realm inside your head, and that mental world, that realm within theirs. The inability to tap into that other realm with completeness means that you are not connected, that you are alone. This journey that you are on is YOUR journey, and it is composed of a unique line of experiences. Thus, **part of the answer to that question of "Who am I?" is that you are someone on a journey.** All that you experience will be your experiences, even though you will interact constantly with others. What goes into your brain from even shared experiences is never what goes into their brains. As someone once asked me back when I was in college, "When you go six feet under, how many people are going to jump into your grave with you?" I looked at him puzzled as to where he was going with this and said, "Zero." "Exactly," he replied, "and that's how many people you should be living your life for." It is **your** journey, yet who are you living it for? **Your journey is part of who you are, and, yet, how much of who you are is determined by the permission of others?** You will not suffer a cut and someone else bleeds and feels the pain. I am over-emphasizing the uniqueness of "you," but the point is, your physical body and your experiences are part of the answer to the question of "Who am I?"

What part does the body play in that question? You are in your "journey suit," the body that encases all that you are. Blow up a balloon. What does that balloon encase? Air from your lungs. That balloon is a container of your "essence," and just as that balloon contains an element of you, your body contains all of **you**. Now, why do I call your body a "journey suit?" The best analogy that I can give you here is that of the scuba diver. When he goes into the ocean to explore, he puts on a wet suit and an air tank. This enables him to exist in a world that is not his own, a world from which he did not come, a world in which he will not stay, and all of that "journey" beneath the ocean is made possible by that "suit." **So, who am I? I am a body that contains a soul that is on a journey in this plane of existence. I am from another world, I do not come from "here," and I will not stay "here" forever. When this journey is complete, "who I truly am" will return to the place from which "who I truly am" came.**

There are those who cannot grasp the concept of the soul. Look at the common automobile. It does not start up and move without someone getting into it, turning the ignition key, putting it into drive and pressing the gas pedal. This is the inanimate being animated. The automobile has all of the components for action, but all of them are inanimate until an animator comes along and causes activity within their parts. Look at a dead body. What is missing? Life, some will say. Yes, it is missing life, but what is life? Life is a body having activity in its parts. The lungs are inhaling and exhaling, the heart is beating, blood is coursing through the veins, and the brain is thinking. Yet, what is the animator of these otherwise inanimate parts? You. If you do not exist, these parts do not animate, they do not produce anything. Just as the scuba diver goes into a world that is foreign to his own, and he wears a special suit to be able to do so, shedding the suit when he returns to his world of origin, the suit is not the diver. The diver is the diver, and the suit is an illusion to any fish that see the diver. What the fish see when they see a diver is a fish in their world, but the truth is, the diver is not from the sea. You are not from this world, but from another, and the body you wear while here is what makes it possible for you to interact with this world, this plane of existence. **So, importantly, we need to realize that who we are is not what we first begin to think we are, that is, the body we see in the mirror. We will shed that body at the end of our tour in this plane of existence, but who we are will continue to exist somewhere else.**

These two analogies should help you begin to understand that the body is a vehicle. It is animated by you while you are visiting this plane of existence, but it is only part of who you are. In life, it will stare back at you in the mirror, it will be photographed hundreds of times for identification purposes, and your body will be the way everyone recognizes you all through life. But, it is only a portion of who you are. You will pay attention to its needs, feed it when it is hungry, give it sleep when it is tired, and you will find that it enjoys being loved by others. However, all of these are merely physical details, such as when your car needs fuel, an oil change, new brakes. You pay attention to the needs and interests of your body, and what you do to your body also determines to a great deal what futures lie ahead for you. Smoke all of your life, and you may have to endure cancer in your older years. Eat like there is no tomorrow, and you may suffer from the sorrows of obesity. Thus, how we treat our bodies also contributes to what the entity that animates, that resides within, has to endure. How we treat our bodies and minds, therefore, has a direct correlation to what we experience during this journey. Someone once said, "Sad is the person who happiness is measured by the permission of others." Your journey, their limitations. My analogy here would best be described as putting a cage around that scuba diver. Think of all the chains, the weights, and the anchors that have been placed on you by others. Because we interact with other human beings all of our lives, those interactions become another part of the question, "Who am I?" Thus, when someone asks this question, the answer is that you are more than one simple name. You are a complex amalgam of parts, the physical body, the immediate contributions to your personality by your family and friends, your environmental influences and events that happen to you each and every day, all of these contribute to the shaping of who you are perceived to be physically. But, there is a second part to who you are, and that is the part of you that resides seemingly invisible within that body. **Your soul. That nebulous entity that is the animator of the physical body is the permanent "you."** The physical parts of "you" will age and die, turn to dust, as we say, but the real "you" will step out of that prison of clay and walk away from the wreckage, unaffected by death, and carrying within it all of the memories of this life. So, who am I?

I am two beings wrapped together for life, my physical being and my eternal soul. My body is an actor on a stage, and my soul is the true identity of that actor.

Still, let's add some complexity to the equation.

There is a metaphysical agreement between the body and the soul. The Creator Force put that into the equation for a reason. The difference between the analogy of the scuba diver and the human swimming under the sea is that the scuba suit does not change with the experience, while the human body not only changes with life, the way it experiences and adapts to life's challenges adds to the memories of the soul, and when the soul steps out of the body for the last time to journey on to the next plane of existence, it does take with it all of the memories of every experience in this life. Thus, there is a constant interplay between the body, the "suit," and the soul, the "observer," the true eyes behind the eyes. How often have you felt that, when you look into someone's eyes, you are looking into something very deep? It is because you are looking into the soul. We are sent here to this plane of existence for a reason, and the "suit" was designed to contribute to the final totality of the experience. **We "experience" until our last breath is taken.**

What we are taught sets the stage for many of our quests in life. The Crusaders, for example, thought that they had a heavenly mandate, but what was it that prepared them in their early years to make them susceptible to such religious ambitions? **Our early years are at the hands of "others." Those "others" tell us what they believe, and we simply choose to accept their beliefs as our own, growing more intent on following and enforcing those beliefs as we grow, or, we eventually separate from the beliefs of those who were our early teachers, find new ones, and change our earlier ideas and ideals accordingly.** All of these experiences constitute our "path," that path being part of the "Why am I here?" question that I will discuss later.

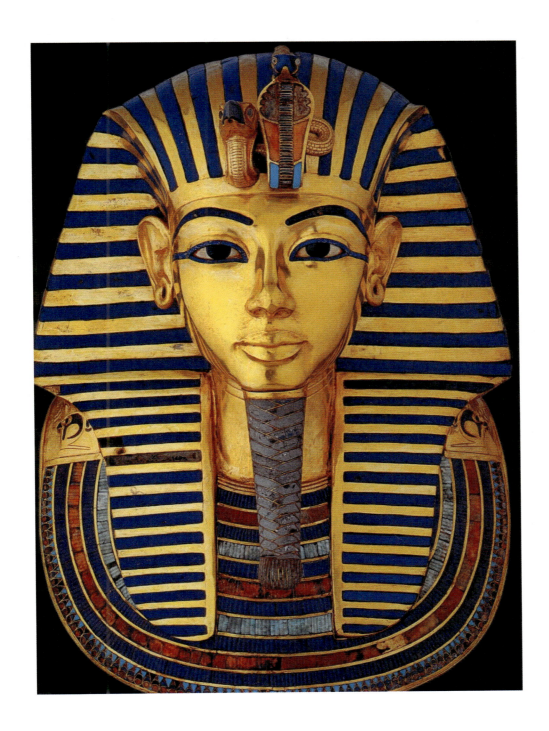

I am two beings wrapped together for life, my physical being and my eternal soul. My body is an actor on a stage, and my soul is the true identity of that actor.

How often have you felt that, when you look into someone's eyes, you are looking into something very deep? It is because you are looking into the soul.

What are some of the things that we are taught? The foods that we are fed as a child become the mainstay of our diets. The religion in which we are raised becomes a guiding set of principles by which we tend to make decisions. The group of people in our immediate society tend to become those whom we find attractive for romantic pursuits. The schools in which we matriculate teach us the societal "norms" by which we strive to fit in. And there is so much more that we call experiences, from loving parents to parents who fought constantly, from having many brothers and sisters to being an only child, from being rich to being poor, from being popular to being unwanted, all of these are the many facets of the diamond that is being formed into the entity that we call "Me." And though all of these factors began as unavoidable circumstances, because we were children being reared in whatever environment we entered as we came here, all of these factors will eventually become choices as we come to realize that our parents are not who we came "**from**," but who we came "**through**." **Our parents were merely the doorway through which we entered into this plane of existence.** Once we begin to realize who "we" really are, once "me" begins to want to be free from the constraints of others, a new set of experiences begins. This, then, is where we either stay a "child" for life, remaining under the domination of others who set our limitations, or, it is where we break the unnecessary chains with which they tried to shackle us, and we go in search of the answers to the Four Questions. **It is only when we truly set out to find the answer to "Who am I?" that we finally begin to live life fully.**

If I placed a dark mask over your eyes for your first twenty years of life, a mask which permitted absolutely no light to get through, then I removed that mask and let you see the real world, the enlightenment would be staggering and astonishing. Such is death. The human body has its limitations, and once the physical limitations of this human body are removed, and we pass out of the human body into the next plane of existence, it will be fascinating to experience that awakening.

Why are we limited to our inabilities? Why, for instance, can we not see past death? Why can we not understand where all that we see came from? Why is there even death? Why is there suffering and pain? Why are there evil people? The answer is simple: We did not write the play.

I once had a life-changing experience while I was in college. It came to me while I was in church, and I had reached a point where I needed answers that I was not getting from my church, or even from my religion. To make a long story short, I walked out of that church service, disgusted and disillusioned, and I said to myself, "There is no God!" I went back to my room in the dormitory, and I could not sleep, such was the pressing urgency of finding an answer to the main question, "Does God exist?" I had been raised in a Fundamentalist religion, deeply religious, and I was a zealot among zealots, an absolutely religious fanatic. But, I had been troubled by what I was discovering, and I felt that God was not listening. Since he had not answered, He did not exist; that was my reasoning. However, inquiring minds need to know what to believe. Fairy tales don't work when you are intelligent. There I lay on my bed, the door locked, the lights turned out, so that no one would knock on my door and interrupt this emergency meeting of myself and reality. I began by asking myself if I even existed. After considering that I might merely be a figment of someone else's imagination, a participant in some dream, I went back to a foundational building block of philosophy: "Cogito ergo sum," "I think, therefore, I am." Because I am thinking, I exist. But, what next?

I knew that there was a world beyond my dormitory window. People in China, halfway around the world, were having a life regardless of my denial or acknowledgement of their existence. Their world went on, with or without me. This world was, therefore, greater than just me. It was not some figment of "my" imagination, and I was just a very small piece of something very large. But, did I create this world? Foolish sounding, but why could I not say that all of this was merely my imagination? I looked at the tree outside of my window. Could I create that tree? Could I simply say, "Let a tree appear here or there," and it would happen? No, a resounding no! I could plant it and watch it grow, but I could not make it appear out of nowhere. I went back to a foundation of physics, and that is, nothing can be created or destroyed. For the uneducated who say, "Well, if I set fire to that piece of paper, I have destroyed it," the answer right out of the physics book they forgot to read is simply this: you did not destroy that piece of paper. You separated its elements. Every last atom that was in that paper is still here, just in various other states now. You rearranged molecules, but you destroyed nothing. So, just as I cannot speak that tree, or anything else, into existence, and since I cannot destroy it, I, therefore, do not have that power. Yet, that tree exists. Clouds exist. The sun exists. I have no memory of having ever created them, and I know that I do not have the power to create them. If I do not have this power, and they do exist, then something greater than myself created these things. And as I reasoned in my dormitory room, I came to the conclusion that there is a force greater than myself, a force that created all that I see, even created me. All down through history, humans have tried to name this force, and all of the various gods have worn the name, but one thing is very clear, **this Creator Force is the author of the play in which we find ourselves.**

Ancient Statue of Zeus

Here is the sad part. As human beings down through the ages had wrestled with this conundrum, they have created ways that the Creator Force should be worshipped, because, as ancient civilizations thought, any sorrow, any pestilence, any earthquake, was a sign that the Creator Force, however they named it, was displeased by something they had done. They had to find how to please the god or gods, and religion was born. Look back through history, and look at all of the religions that have come and gone. Every religion is an attempt to define the Creator Force, to give that entity a personality, and, in most cases, to give it a human from. We call this anthropomorphism. Using just the Christian Bible, for example, we see reference after reference of God sitting on a throne, getting angry or jealous, seeing with His eyes, listening with His ears, walking on His feet, touching with His hands, all human attributes. The average human being thinks of God as a man sitting on a throne with unlimited powers, much in the same way ancient Greeks thought of Zeus. We humans like to think that God looks like us. There was a time when we thought of the sun as a god, the moon was a goddess, and there was a pantheon of gods and goddesses, depending on which "religion" you subscribed to, that covered every facet of every experience we encountered. If it thundered, well, that was the activity of the gods. When it rained, once again, the gods. From the fertility of the crops to a baby delivered alive, the gods. Every civilization, every period in history, there are religions that have come and gone, and they all had in common their need to explain the unexplained in the best way that their minds could. I see embalmed pharaohs, entombed Chinese emperors, even mummified remains of indigenous tribes here in the Americas, and there was one thing that was constant among them: their bodies were prepared for an afterlife. There were religious rituals that were performed, and for what? Their religions taught that there was life after death, life with the gods. If there is one thing that should be apparent to thinking and intelligent people, it is this: **Truth is immutable, all else is myth.** Thus, part of our life experience should be to separate ourselves from myth and learn Truth.

Back in 1992, I wrote: "If any man finds a truth and teaches that truth to others, those to whom he teaches will be in such awe of the truth that they will attempt to deify the person who teaches the truth, rather than live the learned truth. They will build temples to this man solely because he taught a truth, and they will make rituals by which to honor him, but will still not be living the learned truth. And in these temples, they will appoint keepers of the ritual and will devise ways to force others to observe the requirements of the temple. They will keep the truth in a box covered with layer upon layer of gold and silk, yet all who see it shall not see truth, but, merely gold and silk."

I often tell people that Truth is a giant tapestry on which is a beautiful picture. And there are those who will run up to it, pluck a thread or two and run with that in their hands, exclaiming, "I have the Truth!" No, what they have is a thread. Truth is the entire picture, not just one or two threads. Unfortunately, most religions are based on a thread or two of truth, and the rest of what they teach is "threads" that did not come from the Truth. Let's examine some ancient beliefs that were based on probably less than even a thread.

There is no religion, ancient or current, that does not reflect those who founded it. Religions can be followed by a handful of adherents, or millions, and these religions can be local or worldwide in their membership. All religions begin with someone trying to find the answers to the four questions, then, somewhere along the way, they stop listening and start talking, and it seems that, once they start talking, they end the quest for the Truth right there and begin the elaborate process of wrapping their findings in gold and silk. One common theme I have seen throughout the centuries is the predominance of male chauvinism. For example, in the Bible, the story of Sodom and Gomorrah is a classic, well-loved by anti-gay bigots who erroneously like to cite this story as God's disgust with homosexuals, which, of course, is completely false and wishful thinking on their part. Regardless of what one thinks of the story, one does not have to be able to read Hebrew to translate the male chauvinism contained therein, because one of the most glaring examples is when Lot offers his two daughters to the men of the city to dissuade them from harming his male guests. "Take my two virgin daughters, but don't touch these men." And when Lot flees the city, he is warned not to look back. Thus, when Lot's wife looks back, she is turned into a pillar of salt, but when Lot does so, he sees the city in smoke and nothing happens to him... because he is a male. Even in the second chapter of Genesis, wherein it lists the order of Creation, we find that the male race, "ha adam" in Hebrew, is created first. Contrary to

Here is a 15th Century Persian painting depicting the prophet Mohammed, accompanied by Gabriel, and they are riding on the back of Buraq, a horse-like mythical creature. Here, they are visiting Hell where they see "shameless women" who are being punished eternally. Their "sin"? Exposing their hair so that strangers could see it, which incited lust in the men. The women are strung up by their hair and burned forever.

In this painting, Mohammed sees women in Hell whose crimes were mocking their husbands and leaving their homes without the permission of, you guessed it, their husbands. They are hanging by hooks through their tongues and are being burned for eternity. No messing around, a large part of religion is about scaring people into subjection.

what unscholarly people love to think, "ha adam" is not some man named Adam. According to the Creation account in Genesis, for a long time, the male race is all there is. Eventually, God decides to create animals and bring them to "ha adam" to see what mankind thinks of them. Still, no women. After all, it's a man's world. At least that's the way the male chauvinists felt when they authored these books. Women were less than cattle in value. So, God first created the male race, then He created the animals, and after another interval of time, God created the female race, "ha ishah." And, no, this was not some singular woman named Eve, which name does not appear in this Creation story. So, you have the male race created, then you have the animals created, and finally, you have the female race created. Here is a puzzle for you. If there were only two people created, where did the sons of Adam and Eve get their wives?

All through the Bible and Christian history, Old Testament right on through the New Testament, women were subjugated to the role of being inferior to men. Progressive societies have managed to get rid of this absurdity while regressive societies have reveled in it. And since religions have borrowed from one another down through the ages, we cannot blame religions for male chauvinism. The blame goes directly to the ones who have predominantly controlled the narrative, the male race. Thus, when we read religious literature, we see two prominent features: it is written for the benefit of men, and the codes of conduct are always addressing the time and culture that was in vogue when that writing took place. Looking at the conduct of the Christian church, for example, people tend to think that the Christian church of today is a mirror of the Early Church, and nothing could be further from the truth. The attire of the beginning of Christianity was Roman and Greek, and that culture dictated much of what was being written. What was appropriate for men and women to wear in A.D. 40 would have no resemblance to what was considered "Christian" centuries later, no matter how much people think they are interpreting the Bible correctly for their day and time. Joan of Arc was burned at the stake primarily for wearing men's attire. This is typical of male chauvinists using the Bible as their tool. When we look at these absurdities, we tend to discredit the relative religions, when what we should be doing is separating out the threads, looking for the threads that belong in the tapestry of Truth and discarding the rest. Obviously, religious edicts that were written to keep women "in their place" have no relationship to the answers to our quest for Truth. Furthermore, the question of "Who am I?" is not a value question whose answer is dependent on whether or not you are male. Throw two pieces of wood into a stream, and they are both going to float downstream toward some future destiny, and even though they are both going to interact with different currents and rocks in the stream, they will both go in virtually the same direction, because they are both wood. The stream's current will affect them both with the same physics. It is the forces of the stream that they will encounter and respond to as they occur, and the same is to be said of life. Male or female, the individual is subjected to the exact same metaphysical forces. It is only the randomness and timing of these events that changes the response. For example, a pair of biological twins, one male and one female, are leaving their house to go for a walk. A car driving by loses control and swerves into them hitting the male. The female was farther away from the car and was not struck. Though they are both human, and, in this case, within the same time and place on their journey through life, only the male was hit. The female will be impacted in other ways than the male. He was physically impacted, she was psychologically impacted. He might die from his injuries, she might live another forty years. So, my point here is that the question of "Who am I?" is not one that should first be answered by gender, even though this will play some part in a person's destiny. Who I am is not, first of all, whether I am male or female, but what role I play in this plane of existence relative to others who exist around me. We are interacting in a play that was written by someone greater than ourselves.

These photos are NOT to ridicule, but to ASK, and the question is simply this: Can all of these opinions be right? Is there only one right answer, and all the rest are false? If only one way is correct, then which one is right? Or, is ANY of this required by God? And WHO thought up these commandments for religious attire?

To find the answers to who we are, some of the purpose for why we are here, we need to separate much of our religious beliefs from the search, because far too much of what we use to identify the false illusion of who we are is based on religions that are greatly mankind-manufactured. One analogy that I often give is to tell someone, if I paint that window black, and I then tell you that the sun no longer shines, you have two choices: believe what I tell you, or go and scrape the paint off of that window. But whether you believe me, or you go and scrape the paint off of that window, the sun still shines. Truth can stand to be questioned, lies cannot. No one should ever be afraid to question, especially when it comes to life and eternity. Currently, I live in an area that is heavily populated by Amish. On any given day, I will see not just children, but adults, pedaling along on scooters. The reason for this is that their religion forbids the use of bicycles. And every time I see one of them slowly moving down the road, I have a number of thoughts that go through my head, such as how much of this wondrous world they will never see or experience, because someone many centuries ago said that their happiness should be constrained by his permission. They must ride in horse-drawn buggies, not cars, they may not fly in airplanes, and they cannot even ride a bicycle. He painted their windows black, and many of them have never thought to go over and scrape the window to see if that is paint or Truth. Who has control of YOUR life? And if someone other than yourself controls you, then why did you give them permission? As one of my friends back at the university used to say, "How many of those people are going to jump into your grave with you?" None of them are going to jump into your grave and go along with you when you die, so why have you given them control? **Truth should control your life.**

Thus, the question of "Who am I?" is complex, because before we can discover the answer to that question, we must remove the layers of "interference" that were painted on our outer walls by others, we must break the chains that bind us to superstitions and useless anchors, and we must lose the fears that others put there to keep us in line with their fears.

When we remove the useless and unproductive weights that hold us down, we find that what remains is the being that the Creator Force designed, this human being, this actor on the stage of life and its true identity. Our true identity, the soul, is what we actually are. The suit we wear around it, the body, is the product of where we are in this time on Earth. **Much like a diamond that receives color from the compression of the forces that surrounded it during its creation, our souls are colored by the forces of this existence.** We will leave this plane of existence colored by the very experiences that we went through, all the loves and the heartaches, the joys and the sorrows, the gains and the losses, all that we have come through will be the seed for the next life. But, if we came here from somewhere else, then that should lead us to the second question of the four, "Where did I come from?"

Where Did I Come From?

   The second of the four questions, "Where did I come from?", is not easily answered, because the proofs for any conclusion are severely lacking. Oh, we can show our lineage charts, talk about parents and grandparents, DNA, and a host of other genetic factors, but always keep in mind that you did not come "from" your parents, you came "through" your parents. They were your doorway into this plane of existence. Yes, you are part of their biological essence, and your body is most definitely a byproduct of their genes, but "you," the real "you" is not the body, but the soul. Remember, the body is merely the suit that, like the scuba gear for the ocean diver, allows you to "submerge" into this plane of existence for the time that you are to visit here. Saying that your origin is your parents is like saying that the store where you picked up your scuba gear is your point of origin. **You existed before you took possession of the suit.**

   We, as humans, tend to think of ourselves as large items in the scale of life, but take a look at the universe. When we stare out into space on a starry night, the sheer vastness of space ought to indicate that, in the visual

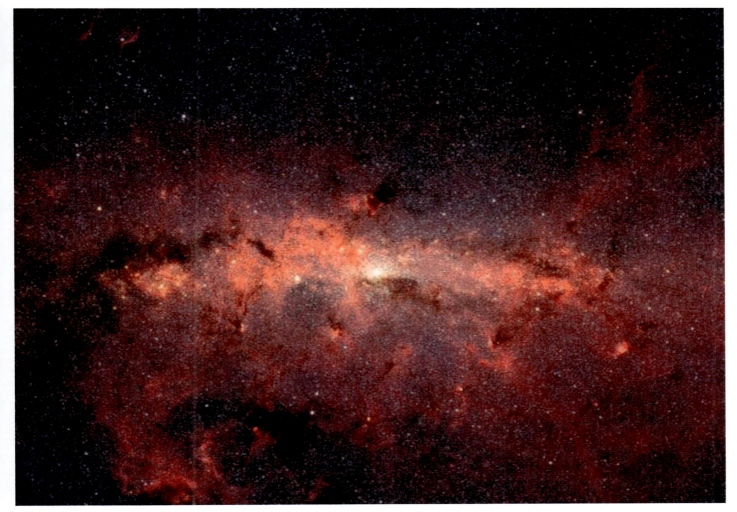

   In this photo from NASA, here is a view of the starry core of our spiral Milky Way. To give you an idea of the immensity of this, pick any two white dots, and you would not be able to go from one to the other in your lifetime, even if you were traveling at the speed of light, such is the distance between them. Now, how big do you really think you are in all of this?

scale of things, we are not as big and important as we like to think we are. Life here on Earth is more like a bunch of living creatures in a terrarium. Look at that terrarium from the outside of the enclosure, and their world looks small, but to those creatures that inhabit it, that terrarium and everything inside of it is a vast world of daily challenges and rewards. When we consider this giant planet on which we live relative to the universe that surrounds us, we can readily see how small our planet is in the equation. Knowing this, our relative size to what is out there in space, one can look inward with a myopic view that blinds them to the "more" that is out "there," one can even ignore what is out "there," but, as I stated earlier in this book, I can paint the window black and tell you that the sun no longer shines, and you can take my statement as truth, or you can scrape the paint off that window and see the truth for yourself. Regardless of the view you take, the truth will still exist outside of that window, and regardless of the approach you take with regard to human beings in relationship to the universe, **beyond your little world on this planet, there are other planes of existence.**

It would amaze some people to learn that Earth, our solar system, the Milky Way galaxy and the galaxies beyond the Milky Way, called the Local Group, all of this mass is moving through this other plane of existence at the rate of 400 miles per second. Where are we going? What is pulling, or pushing, us "there?" Of course, even at that awesome speed, relative to distances out there between these other spatial objects in the vast distances, we are never going to run into any of those objects in our lifetimes, because everything in space that scientists are able to observe and calculate is expanding, moving outward and away from us, even though there are realms out there that are not expanding at the same speed. The fact that all of the universe is moving away from a "point" in time is as if everything that exists was the product of some great explosion. There is a force propelling "all that is" in an outward direction. Thus, the Big Bang Theory. Something began all of "this," and that something is the Creator Force. Since we did not create a single thing on this planet, it goes without saying that we did not create anything we see out there in space, either, and just looking at all of that immensity, that vastness, the masses of those great objects in the faraway distances, we are nothing compared to the creation of those immeasurable objects, which further intensifies the difference between our **powerlessness** and the **powerfulness** of the Creator Force. **We cannot even begin to fathom all there is to know about these objects in outer space, yet the Creator Force designed them. Think on this long and hard. It should help to keep you humble.**

And the Creator Force made this home for us, our own little terrarium. Think of its uniqueness. We have hot days, cold days, but it is always at a temperature that we can live with, yet the temperature "out there" in space is minus 455 degrees Fahrenheit. That should make you a little more inquisitive as to why this anomaly known as Earth even exists, because it is just right for our species and all others that share this planet. An analogy would be to think of us as something akin to sparks from a great flame. Build a bonfire at night when it is very dark, get the flames going really well, then stir the fire. What happens? You see sparks fill the night sky as they race upward on some unseen force, spiraling into an eventual emptiness as other sparks take their place. The life of each spark is seemingly short by our estimations, lasting only a few seconds before going from brilliant white to dull orange to complete blackness. But, in that short span of time, that spark has gone through many chemical reactions and changes, atoms have spun off from molecules, and energy has been released. As Physics teaches us, nothing is created or destroyed, only changed, so that the original piece of wood has not been burned up, rather, it has been changed into other components. All of the atoms that were present in that original tree were present in that change of firewood into sparks and ash. What once began as a piece of living wood, was cut down and turned into dry firewood, and that piece of dry firewood was heated until it ignited into flames, and those flames produced more chemical reactions until those embers were stirred by you, and up went a flurry of sparks. Each of those sparks was a world for a brief moment in time, a rapidly changing

world in which the amount of chemical actions would astound you. How long is long, and how short is short? If one of those sparks that is seen flying upward from that bonfire is a tiny world, and we think, compared to our lifespans, that it only lasts for a few seconds, thus, it cannot have any significance, then think on this: the Creator Force was here before we even existed. Measured against the length of time the Creator Force has been around, how long is the lifespan of Earth and its inhabitants? I liken our existence to a fishbowl in a tornado. We are spinning around in a cosmic force that is beyond our comprehension, yet something is protecting our fishbowl. That protective force was designed intentionally, just as everything we see around us was designed intentionally. The same force that created that fishbowl also created that tornado. We, therefore, obviously emanate from the Creator Force, and Earth is speeding through that "tornado" of black matter and microwave energy in outer space at the exciting speed of 400 miles per second. We are moving away from our origin at an exciting clip, just like those sparks rise excitedly above the bonfire in the night, and the analogy should be clear - **We come from a source of great energy, but it is an energy with unfathomable intelligence. This force, the Creator Force, inhabits all that ever has been, all that is, and all that ever will be. And when you ask, "Where did I come from?", the answer is quite simple: You came from the mind of the Creator Force.**

Just like that wood that grew from a seed, then became a tree, then came to the day it was cut down and dried for firewood, then experienced the day a fire was lit and it began another chemical reaction that changed it into other elements, carbon and oxygen and a host of other atoms were released to join other atoms and become air and ash and water, just as that wood began as something else and became something other, **our lives on earth began somewhere else, as something else, and this journey here is only one of many changes into many other "atoms" in the great cosmos created by the Creator Force.** As I said earlier, the "play" was written by the Creator Force. We are actors on this stage, but we did not write the play. And like those sparks that emanate and rise from the bonfire, we will bounce against each other, race alongside of some and never meet others, yet we will all rise from the bonfire to the sky and finally to our end as sparks. **We will become something else once we change.**

Many people do not want to think back further than their immediate ancestors. It is too hard on their brains to peer back into space and time and look beyond the simple and into the complex. For them, where did I come from is quite simple: my parents. **But, remember once again, you came "through" your parents, not "from" your parents. They were merely the doorway you used to come here. They are not the source of your "soul," your true being. Just as a living tree became firewood, and firewood became sparks, your eternal soul began its existence long before you met your parents.** All down through recorded history, people have had out-of-body, near-death experiences. While their bodies stayed right here, their souls traveled to another place, a place unavailable to the human body, but obviously a place available to the real "you," your soul. I know, because I had just such an experience, and it proves to me that **the human body is a "scuba suit" that our parents helped create, but the soul existed before that suit was ever made, and even though it will borrow that suit for a short time, it will leave that suit at the prescribed time and go to the "next level" of existence, the next plane of existence, the change that comes.** This belief alone has led many to suggest the possibility of reincarnation, coming back to this plane of existence to live on Earth again for a variety of reasons. The belief in reincarnation is not new, nor is it indigenous to any one race, culture or religion. It has permeated every religion on Earth, including Christianity. Let's face it, the idea of reincarnation is very present within the fabric of the "why we are here" theories. And whether you believe in reincarnation or not, just as some of those sparks do fall back into the fire to become heated and active once again, there have been some very convincing studies that show that we, too, may recycle through this plane of existence for reasons genuinely and truly known only to the author of this all, the Creator Force.

What purpose is there for any of us to live another life here? For those religions that teach reincarnation as fact, they say that we come back to live here mainly to "get it right," to pay for "karma debts," to do penance for unjust living in the past life. Some think it is to grow more spiritual until life in this plane of existence is no longer necessary. These teach that there are successive reincarnations at the higher levels beyond Earth, in the realm with "God." These also teach that, at the end of that upward spiral of successive reincarnations, we ultimately re-unite with the Creator Force, becoming one with God, so to speak. For those Christians who do not think Christians ever taught this belief, I point them to two passages in the Bible. In John, Chapter 1, Verses 1 & 2, we read where Jesus and His disciples came upon a man who had been blind from birth: "Now as Jesus was passing by, He saw a man blind from birth, and His disciples asked Him, 'Rabbi, who sinned, this man or his parents, that he was born blind'?" The disciples were following a common belief of karmic debt, that someone had done wrong in a past life, and they were paying for it in this life. Thus, the question they asked is simple to understand, this man is paying a horrible price, that is, he is born blind through seemingly no fault of his own. Being born blind, then, was it his fault, or did his parents do something wrong? The ancient Jewish belief was based in the concept that anyone worshipping other gods would be punished. In Exodus 20:5, we read: "You shall not bow down to them or worship them; for I, the LORD your God, am a jealous God, visiting the iniquity of the fathers on their children to the third and fourth generations of those who hate Me." In this belief, reincarnation was not the factor, punishment of your children was the "scare." **But, if you were no longer in existence, then what did it matter?** In Matthew 16:13-14, we read, "Now when Jesus came into the district of Caesarea Philippi, he asked his disciples, 'Who do people say that the Son of Man is?'

And they said, 'some say John the Baptist, others say Elijah, and others Jeremiah or one of the prophets.'"
Now, if Jesus did not know that the general population believed in reincarnation, why then would He ask His disciples what historical religious figure He was the reincarnation of? If the people did not believe in reincarnation, no one would suggest that He was the reincarnation of Elijah, or anyone else for that matter. So, this belief has been around for a very long time. However, it was forcibly removed from the teachings and beliefs of the Church in A.D 553 when the Roman emperor Justinian called the Fifth Ecumenical Council. In this event, the church teachings were consolidated into a more singular Theology, and the teachings of reincarnation were declared anathema and heresy. It was not overnight, but in the centuries to come, through the use of torture and killings, the Church effectively removed reincarnation from the beliefs accepted by Christians. Nonetheless, **whether we believe in reincarnation or one life, our source of origin is the same—the mind of the Creator Force.**

In our journey of discovery to the answers, what we see thus far is this:

Who am I? I am two beings wrapped together for life, my physical being and my eternal soul. My body is an actor on a stage, and my soul is the true identity of that actor.

Where did I come from? I came from a source of great energy, but it is an energy with unfathomable intelligence. This force, the Creator Force, inhabits all that ever has been, all that is, and all that ever will be. Thus, when you ask, "Where did I come from?", the answer is quite simple:

> You came from the mind of the Creator Force.

This leads us, then, to the next question of the four, Why am I here?

Why Am I Here?

    When we are young, we all like to think that we are going to change the world, that we are going to be rich and famous and have glamorous lives. We'll have it all, and we'll live past 100 years and never look old. Then, reality gradually sets in. Repeating that old Amish saying, "We grow too soon old and too late smart," it isn't long before our dreams run into reality, when we find out that parents bury their children, that homes can burn to the ground, tornados take away even good people, and bears can eat us. Suddenly, the protective bubble that we lived in is revealed for the illusion that it always was, and we want answers to why all of this happens. The young boy who was going to become a movie star ends up working for an insurance company, the young girl who was going to be a famous singer ends up teaching in a school for the handicapped. What we thought was to be our destiny becomes a long forgotten dream that awakens from time to time, brings a smile and is put back in the photo album of memory. We eventually resign ourselves to the "me" that our lives became. This is me, this is where I am now, this is who I am. All that I have been through, all that I have learned, all that I have experienced, this is me now. With the time that is left, I will enjoy the memories, I will look to make a few new ones, and, as I reach the point where I have more yesterdays than I have tomorrows, I will ask myself occasionally, "Why am I here?" Eventually, we should know why we were here.

    We absolutely come here for a purpose. The complete answer to the question of what that purpose is may be known only to the Creator Force, but, there is a purpose to our lives, nonetheless. **From the lowest street urchin to the highest king, there is purpose in <u>all</u> lives.** No one is a zero, every life has worth, and the Creator

Force made no mistakes. You have value, and you have a reason for existing. But why are "YOU" existing? Where do "YOU" fit in to the world that is all around you? What is your part? What do you contribute?

As insignificant as you may think yourself to be, you do contribute to the totality of life. Equally, why all the misfortunes that befall you? It has often been said that bad things happen so that we can appreciate the good things that happen, which is an over-simplification of things, but bears inspecting as a theory. I come to this point because there are so many who will ask, "Why do bad things happen to good people?" "Why is there evil in the world?" I remember my father's sister once saying to me, "The only Hell is the one right here on Earth." One only has to study the Holocaust and the atrocities of Nazi Germany during World War II, to look at film footage of those poor, innocent human beings who were tortured and murdered in ways that defy sanity, to then ponder and puzzle over how this inhumanity could ever happen. Human beings torturing fellow human beings? Why? That war was evil, the people who started it were evil, the people who tortured others during that war were evil, so why did this happen? Why did the Creator Force allow all of this? Was it by design? Was there some purpose for allowing it to happen?

One theory is that we are all put here with intrinsic value, but we are also given free will, and that free will can take the gift of life and invest it wisely, or it can take that same gift and destroy it. **There is a path in all lives that appears, but it has a fork up ahead with one path leading upward and the other path leading downward.** I believe that there is enough of a glimpse of what is ahead in either path for us to get a sense of what lies in that direction. I also believe that we can leave either path at any time and change directions, because all paths are choices that we are forever free to make. Nevertheless, the longer we walk in either of those paths, the more difficult it is to change, because the chasm between the two grows ever wider as we progress forward. Even Adolph Hitler was born an innocent baby, a child who was loved and wanted. However, once he began to ponder the paths that appeared before him, he began to make choices that led to the involvement in the experiences that formed him into the person he became. Like a stone thrown into a still pool of water, the water is disturbed, and ripples radiate outward from that disturbance. Hitler's life disturbed the fabric of history, much like the size of the stone thrown into the pool of water determines the wake. This, then, leads us to contemplate - was Hitler an intention of the Creator Force? Or was Hitler a result of collective free choices? You see, Hitler could have been stopped long before he destroyed the lives of millions of human beings, but the collective society that saw him rising did not intervene. Was the collective society too involved with their own personal pursuits to take the time to pay attention to what he was doing and declare him dangerous? Was the collective society too selfish and gullible? Did they want to believe his lies? And, if so, were they reaping what they sowed?

Hitler was presented paths as he grew up, and the paths he chose gave rise to the paths he offered his fellow citizens. Those who chose to follow Hitler created more paths, each of them leading to experiences that others now saw before them. **We are all pebbles and stones being thrown into the pool of life, and our "waves" rippling outward affect other lives.** Just as there is evil in this world, there is also good, and those who have chosen the path that leads upward to spiritual enlightenment can also mass in numbers sufficient to march against evil and subdue it. Thus, when Hitler's atrocities grew to alarm the good people of the world, they massed into a force that ultimately destroyed Hitler's regime. For those who gave their lives fighting against Hitler, such was the purpose of their existence. Are evil people sent to cause us to get involved? To fight against evil and, thus, become stronger in that which is good? When you lift weights to strengthen your muscles, it is resistance that causes muscle to grow, without which the muscle would atrophy and weaken. **Perhaps** the Creator Force designed Earth as a metaphysical training ground where we come to grow into greater beings. If so, then it would explain the presence of every challenge we face., because we are molded by adversity. Those who were incarcerated and tortured during the Holocaust never forgot their experiences, and they formed a powerful force for good when they were freed.

When a person places two magnets together, if the poles of equal polarity are aligned directly against each other, they will repel each other with a seemingly invisible force. What is this force? It is invisible to the naked eye, yet it can be felt, and it does exert a tangible quality. Likewise, when the poles of opposite polarity are brought together, they will attract very strongly and bond. Once again, there is a seemingly invisible force pulling them together. The same can be said for the causes of forward propulsion in our lives. We are affected by the negative and the positive events in our lives mutually. If no one in our family ever died, we would never know sorrow, and we would not value our time with them as much as we would if we knew death. Experiencing the shock and loss that death brings to our lives causes us to no longer take the remaining members of our circle for granted. We now want to hold them tighter. Good and evil, life and death, the forces that cannot exist without the other, in the world of the magnets, opposites attract, they bond, form a union that is difficult to pull apart. It is true that we cannot have a life of completely one without the other, and the Creator Force designed it this way for a reason. Just as there is strength in a magnetic bond, there is strength in the bond of good and evil, or happiness and sorrow, being played out as they should. When we laugh from the bottoms of our hearts, and when we cry from the same place, we have gained something from the experience, we have grown from it, and we are forever further ahead in our journey and its purpose.

Our true essence, our true being, the soul, is shaped by our experiences here. I have often said that, when we leave this physical body behind at death, we will take with us all of the memories that we made while here on Earth. Whether you believe in reincarnation or not, there are some metaphysical things that cannot be explained any other way, but that we may well indeed have lived before. I have studied reincarnation extensively, and there are many quality, scientific books available on the subject for those who wish to study some of the evidence. One example that always comes to mind when I discuss this subject with people is of a well-documented case recalled in the scholarly book, The Case For Reincarnation by Joe Fisher, about a young girl named Romy Crees in Des Moines, Iowa. From the time she was able to talk, she insisted that she was Joe Williams, the husband of Sheila Williams and the father of three children. She detailed how she had died in a motorcycle accident. These memories were so persistent that her parents decided to have a session with Hemendra Banerjee, a professional investigator of "extracerebral memory." It was winter, 1981, when Banerjee and his research assistant wife, Marjit, along with two journalists from the Swedish magazine Allers, arrived at the home of the Crees family. Romy's mother, Bonnie, told them that she had tried to distract her daughter, Romy, from these memories, hoping that they would pass, and her daughter could get on with a "normal" life. However, nothing stopped the memories Romy was having, and Bonnie, a devout Catholic, was at wits end. Little Romy told them that she had gone to school in Charles City, that she lived in a red brick house and had married Sheila and had children. She recounted how her mother had a pain in her leg and showed everyone where the pain was. Romy went on to recount an event where she had started a fire, and her mother had put it out by throwing water on it, but burned her hand in the process. Romy told everyone that she wanted to go to Charles City and tell her mother that she was okay. It was decided to go to Charles City and investigate the details that Romy had given. The group, which now included Dr. Greg States and Barry Crees, Romy's father, headed for Charles City, 140 miles away. Without even knowing how close they were to their destination, Romy climbed into the front seat and said, "We have to buy flowers. Mother

Williams loves blue flowers. And when we get there, we can't go through the front door. We have to go around the corner to the door in the middle." And here is where facts lay doubts to rest. When they arrived at the house, little Romy pulled Banerjee impatiently up the path to the front door where a printed sign read: "Please Use The Back Door."

At the back door, they rang the door bell, and an elderly woman answered the door. She was leaning on metal crutches. Romy had been correct when she said that they would have to use the back door. She was even further correct when she called the lady Mother Williams and that she had a pain in her leg, because the lady introduced herself as Mrs. Louise Williams, and her right leg was wrapped in a bandage. However, Mrs. Williams did not know these strangers, had a doctor's appointment to go to, and left. Little Romy was in tears. An hour later, the team came back, and, this time, they were successful in gaining an audience with Mrs. Williams. When Mrs. Williams unwrapped the bouquet of blue flowers, she was intrigued and said that her late son's last gift to her was a bouquet of blue flowers. Romy's father, Barry, now related to Mrs. Williams all of Romy's recollections, and Mrs. Williams was astonished at all of the details about her and her family that this little girl knew. Romy had described a red brick house that she had grown up in, and this one was painted white. Mrs. Williams explained that the house had originally been red brick, but it was destroyed in a tornado ten years earlier, and Joe had helped them rebuild it. He was, in fact, the one who insisted that they keep the front door closed in the winter. At some point, Mrs. Williams went into another room to retrieve a photo, and little Romy ran after her. When they returned, Mrs. Williams was clutching a framed photo of her son Joe, his wife Sheila and their three children. The photo had been taken the Christmas before the fatal accident that killed both Joe and his wife Sheila. Mrs. Williams was stunned as she announced to the group that little Romy had recognized all of them, even knew their names and the details of the accident in 1975 that killed Joe two years before Romy was born. Mrs. Williams also confirmed that she had burned her hand putting out a fire that Joe had started when he was younger. Every detail that little Romy gave about their life in Charles City was verified as accurate and true by Mrs. Williams.

When our beliefs system is challenged, we can either run in fear and hide from what we find, or we can approach with wisdom and confidence to explore what we find. I use the example of the Sentinelese, a tribe inhabiting the North Sentinel Island, one of the Andaman Islands in the Indian Ocean. This island is about the size of Manhattan, and the inhabitants, the Sentinelese, have been virtually untouched by modern society for 55,000 years. No one is allowed to make contact with them, and they are observed from the air. These people live in the stone age, and the shock that would come to them is unimaginable if they were exposed to even a fraction of the items that we take for granted in our modern lives. In many ways, we are just like them when it comes to the realm of the metaphysical. It is much more comforting for us to rely on the tales that have been handed down to us, soothing tales that seem to explain how everything works. But, if we used that same methodology, we would not have planes and cars, we would not have telephones and televisions, we would not have hospitals and vaccines, because all of these required that someone look past the hearsay and folk tales and explore truth. As I often say, truth can always stand to be questioned. Only a lie will not stand up to questioning. Those who do not question, who do not explore, who do not dare to go beyond the boundaries set by others, are no better off than the Sentinelese. **I do not think that the Creator Force put us here to be imprisoned, but to experience this plane of existence. To do otherwise would be like taking a vacation to a place you had always wanted to see, then staying in the hotel room the entire time you are there.**

One other example of events that indicate a need to investigate the theories of reincarnation involves the selection of the fourteenth Dalai Lama of Tibet. When the thirteenth Dalai Lama had passed away, the Tibetan monks, who believe completely in the reality of reincarnation, set about searching for his reincarnated entity. They interpreted signs and spiritual visions that would lead them to where he had been reborn. One of those visions was had by a lama, the regent Reting Rinpoche. While meditating at the sacred lake called Lhamo La Tso, he saw a vision of a monastery with a gilded roof and turquoise tiles. He also saw a winding path from that monastery to a hill in the east, opposite of which there was a small house with distinctive eaves. This, he was certain, would be where the child lived. Another sign to the lamas was exhibited by the embalmed corpse of the thirteenth Dalai Lama. His head had been facing south-east, but had turned to face the north-east, thus indicating the direction in which to search for the fourteenth Dalai Lama. With the vision of the sacred lake indicating the Amdo region, and the head of the corpse pointing in that direction, as well, along with other signs that the lamas had been given, the monastery in Amdo was found, and subsequently, the house in which a two-year-old boy was living. The team of lamas that had come to try to locate the fourteenth Dalai Lama visited posing as pilgrims. The leader pretended to be a servant, and had the servants dress as dignitaries, which thus had them spending time with the parents of the boy, while the lama who was heading the exploratory team was then able to sit in the kitchen with the servants of the house. This would allow him to observe the boy without revealing the intentions of the team. The lama held a mala, a Tibetan rosary, in his hands. This mala had belonged to the thirteenth Dalai Lama. The little boy came up to him and asked for it, as if it had belonged to him, and the lama said, "If you know who I am, you can have it." Although the young two-year-old boy had been raised hearing only the Xin Ning dialect spoken in that region, he answered the lama in a perfect Lhasa accent, the accent of the city at the center of Tibetan life, the home of the Dalai Lama, and he told the lama that he was a monk from the Sera monastery, which was completely accurate. No one in that region would have understood the Lhasa accent, and no one knew that this man posing as a servant was actually a highly placed lama from the Sera monastery.

The Dalai Lama as a child.

At this point, the team informed the parents of the little boy that they wanted to test him, because of whom they believed him to be. One of those tests was to place articles owned by the thirteenth Dalai Lama in front of the child, while, at the same time, they placed similar articles that were not. The child picked every item that the thirteenth Dalai Lama had owned and completely disregarded the others. The thirteenth Dalai Lama also had a mole on the inner side of his thigh, and upon examination, the young two-year-old boy had the same mole in the exact same spot. The little boy was eventually taken to the Tibetan capital of Lhasa and installed as the fourteenth Dalai Lama. The rest, of course, is history, but these two examples of reincarnation, as well as the countless others available, tell us that there is more to this metaphysical subject than we have researched. As I stated in my analogy of the painted window, you can believe what someone tells you when they say that the sun no longer shines on the other side of that window, or you can scrape the paint off and see for yourself that the sun is still in existence; therefore, for someone to tell you that reincarnation is a myth, then expect you to simply fall in line and believe them is like

September 1979 - The Mayflower Hotel in Washington, D.C.

I am seen here with His Holiness the Dalai Lama. I had worked tirelessly for two years to get the Carter Administration to allow the Dalai Lama to come to the United States. Obviously, I succeeded.

painting that window black. The truth exists, whether we believe in reincarnation or not, and whether reincarnation is truth or not, examining the subject is not damning. Ignoring the subject is childish, for the simple reason that studying for mental and spiritual enrichment is always rewarding. If the subject is false, it will not stand the test of scrutiny, and proving it false will only help us in our journey toward enlightenment; equally, if it is truth, then, once it has withstood examination, the knowledge can only enrich our existence. Many lives or one life? Neither of these premises changes where I came from, only why I am here.

At the end of your life, you will leave this plane of existence. **What will be obvious is that your entire life was the fulfillment of why you came here.** You lived and died within a set period of time. The Bible says that our death date is set before our birth date. If the counsel of where we exist before here does indeed set that death date, does indeed set the length of time we will spend in this plane of existence, then the end of that period says one thing: **the life we lived may well be what the true purpose was for our existence.**

Exploring the many reasons that add up to the answer to the question of why we are here, one thing does muddy the waters, and that is, what of the people who are born blind, mentally ill, physically impaired in ways that shorten their lifespan, and other such life-interfering conditions, conditions that seem to rob a person of their chance to have a fulfilled life? **And what, then, is a fulfilled life? Is it one that is defined by those who live in this plane of existence, or is it defined by those who dwell beyond this plane of existence?** Without getting into the teachings of predestination, what if we do have conversations with some higher beings before we come to this plane of existence? Much like auditioning for a play, we read the script, we pick out a part we want to play, then we ask to play that role in the play, and those in charge of the play agree to let us play a lead role, a supporting role, or a small role, but we get to be on that stage. The stage, as you will recall, is life, the being who wrote the play is the Creator Force, and our souls inhabit the bodies on that stage. Remember what I told you earlier: **I am two beings wrapped together for life, my physical being and my eternal soul. My body is an actor on a stage, and my soul is the true identity of that actor.**

If we know this, then every character who is on this stage with us, whether their part is a lead role, or some small, seemingly insignificant one, they all become important for their contribution to the telling of this story, this play that was written by the Creator Force. **Whose life has not been altered by time spent with those whose lives seemed otherwise to be insignificant? When we forget ourselves and consider others, then the old biblical statement that it is better to give than to receive finally makes sense.** This is when we truly grow spiritually and metaphysically. We are moved forward when we are challenged, when the rain falls on our heads, when the forest fire approaches, when there is no food to eat, for where there are no challenges, we sit still and stagnate. **A life of purpose is one that is challenged to move to a higher plane, and working to help others who seem to have less than ourselves is one of those challenges.**

Why am I here? To experience.

Where Am I Going When I leave Here?

Ask a Jew, a Christian, a Buddhist, a Muslim or an Atheist, "Where are you going when you leave here?", and the answers will vary, no matter what part of the world they live in at that moment, and their answers are based on what they heard, what they were taught, and sometimes out of frustration, what they have finally given in to. But, none of them will give you the same answer, none of them! How can they all be correct? And when their answers are based on solely what they were exposed to, the best analogy that I can give you is to compare it to someone who has never seen snow. You ask them to describe it, and basically, all they are going to be able to tell you is that it is white and cold, but if they live in equatorial places, they will never be completely accurate, because they only know what they have been told. **When it comes to the afterlife, most people don't even have the benefit of someone showing them a photograph.**

I often say, **"If your Theology conflicts with God's Reality, then you need to revisit your Theology."** What is proven reality should ultimately be the basis for all understanding of the Creator Force. But, what is reality and what is illusion? What have we spent lifetimes deluding ourselves about? What childhood stories have we handed down to our children, who then, in turn, have modified and passed on to the next generation, each religious story gaining in embellishment and sacredness? Baggage that has been handed to you by others is often difficult to unpack... because they threw away the key. **This is one of the reasons so many people have great, secret, internal battles throughout their lives, because they are trying to balance what they are beginning to understand with what they were taught, and they often find that the truth that is revealed to them conflicts with their Easter Bunny stories.** Easter Bunny stories are always so much more cuddly and warm, and for some, they can be heartwarming and reassuring right through the death experience... but for those who think and study, Death is the mouth of a huge black cave that looms directly in front of them, and for these people, the Easter Bunny is no comfort. They want to know the truth. **Where am I going when I leave here?**

Down through the ages, man has created stories of where we are going when we leave this plane of existence. When we study history, there are several facts that come into play here. For one, we all come from a common starting point, but as the centuries passed, we evolved into the various colors, ethnicities, and we even developed a variety of religions. And each of the religions developed a unique outlook on the afterlife, as is significantly evident when we peruse, for example, the vastly different approaches to burying the dead. It is enlightening when we examine how these methods for burying the dead changed over the centuries, and from culture to culture. Observe how the internal organs, including the brain, of the Egyptian pharaohs were put in jars to accompany the mummified bodies. Observe how the Chinese emperors were buried with armies to accompany them in the afterlife. And while Egyptians handled the dead bodies, Tibetans would not think of touching a dead body lest it render them impure. In Tibet, the dead bodies are taken out to be hacked into pieces and fed to the vultures by the outcasts known as the Body Breakers. The rituals for burying the dead throughout history would fill volumes, and all of these rituals were based on religious beliefs. Who was wrong? Who was right? And how many of these rituals survive today? Are they necessary?

A second point to study is that, though we originated from one, we are now so varied in appearances, let alone languages, that we tend to congeal into little groups. Go to any major city and look at "Little Italy," "Chinatown," and a host of other ethnicities that have their own section of the city. Each of these enclaves is formed out of a desire to be with others who look, think and act like themselves. And here's the part we need to magnify - this ethnocentricity causes those in that group to exclude others who are different. Therefore, in the context of world religions, they all teach an exclusion of others. **And in the Afterlife of each religion, notice who is missing - <u>members of other world religions!</u>** So, the description of the Afterlife has not only changed over the centuries, it has evolved according to whatever religion has described it. Furthermore, each religion has a myopic and prejudiced opinion that says that only their belief system is the correct one. But, here is One Great Reality - **All adherents to all the religions since the beginning of time have one thing in common... they all died. Let me say this again. <u>They all died</u>.** Ponder that. Thus, their beliefs did not alter reality, and that reality is, regardless of what they believed, they were destined to leave this plane of existence and travel beyond it to the next plane of existence. That plane of existence is not determined by what

Dressed for death, here are the dried and preserved remains of Bishop Peder Winstrup who died in 1679 in Sweden. For centuries, no one knew that there was a six-month old fetus deliberately concealed under his feet at the bottom of the coffin. Some believe that the baby's body was placed there to ensure that the child made it to Heaven, since it might have been illegitimate and otherwise buried in unsanctified ground.

someone taught you <u>here</u>, but by what has been designed by the Creator Force over <u>there</u>, and regardless of your beliefs, you will go beyond death to experience the ultimate reality - Truth.

Most Christians believe in Heaven and Hell, and they are quick to back up that belief system with biblical scripture. Mao Tse Tung once declared religion to be the "opiate of the masses," and he immediately declared Atheism the religion of the State. Mao saw religion as a tool used by religious institutions to herd people, to use those herds as pawns for the political and power-driven purposes of the leaders of those religious institutions, and he saw no reason to believe any of what these religious people taught. Mao was all about realism, and religion held no allure for him. But what Mao Tse Tung missed was simply this: for each of us, there is a level to life. For some of us, Santa Claus will be real until the day we die, even if that is at the ripe old age of 100, while for others, Santa Claus will disappear at an early age, and we will still be happy in our lives. And for each and every one of us, the sun will still rise in the morning and set at night, and we will live out our lives according to our desires. But, whether we believe in Santa Claus, or whether we disbelieve, that same sun rises and sets, and that same destiny awaits us all... Death and the Afterlife. Death comes to the believer just as surely as it comes for the non-believer. **And here is where the discussion becomes heavy. Atheist, Christian, Buddhist, Muslim, Jew... we all are destined to leave this plane of existence and experience the ultimate, mind-expanding journey into genuine Truth.** <u>Life is the illusion</u>, as the Tibetans teach, but <u>Death is the Truth</u>, and Death will show us realities that, for the most part, we failed to acknowledge.

The Christian Heaven taught by many does not have any room for non-Christians. And this first "bump in the road" causes great debate among even Christians, let alone non-Christians. For example, why would a loving God deprive those who never heard of Jesus the opportunity to live in this paradise? Whatever your response, why were these people not given the opportunity to meet Jesus? As many Christians teach, without a belief in Jesus Christ, there is no entry to Heaven. And for the really legalistic, what about those who came before Jesus was born? Of course, there are arguments about those who were born before the advent of Jesus being "held in reserve" somewhere, awaiting judgment, thus giving them a chance to earn a seat on the bus without the modern requisite of the knowledge of Jesus Christ. All of these arguments are for theological hairsplitters and the legalistic wrangling that reconciling their interpretation of the Bible with questions of reality causes to arise. Here is a simpler approach - throw out all of your pre-conceived ideas, especially those taught by your religious leaders, and start from zero. And here is "zero:" **Every person on this planet was born, and every person on this planet will die.** Let me reiterate that for clarity: We all have the commonality that we were born, and we all have the commonality that we will die. Further, every religion on this planet has tried to figure out what happens after we die, and they all have their ideas on what to expect. Can they all be correct? Let's look at some empirical evidence.

The "abode of the dead" has been described in every known religion since the beginning of recorded history, and elaborate rituals for the preparation for the journey from "here" to "there" fill volumes. Look at the elaborate preparations of the bodies of the ancient Egyptian pharaohs. Look at even the simple burials of ancient Philistines wherein a bottle of perfume was placed next to the head of the deceased. Why? Study the manner in which ancient civilizations sacrificed living humans to appease their gods. Over the many centuries, we have evolved in "what" we sacrifice, but we are still trying to figure out "what" is desired of the "gods." Ancient mythology is filled with elaborate stories of the world beyond this one, and these stories are equally filled with the various ways a human being arrived there. Why are they myths? Why were they so believable in the day and age when they were first concocted, yet, within a few centuries, are relegated to the bins of lore? Century after century, a new religious view is born, evolves, is taught and believed, even defended by wars, then dies out and is later studied in historical documents with intrigue and amusement. And here is a puzzle for you to ponder: where are all those souls? They were born into bodies, and they left those bodies at death. They were taught their beliefs systems, they either believed or disbelieved... and they all died. Millions who were never introduced to the Christian concept of Heaven... where did they go? Think long and hard on this one... where did they go? Don't skip over this point, and don't relegate this one to the bin of "not-sure-but-who-cares?" Where did all of those people who never even heard of **your** religion, who had entirely different ideas on the Afterlife, where did they go? This one thing is common and true... they ALL met Death. Then what?

Of all the world's current religions, I would say that the one that most devotes itself to the studies of death and the world beyond this one would be the religion of Tibetan Buddhism. This is not an endorsement of any one religion, but of all the ones I have studied, I find that Tibetans spend more time dedicating themselves to this search than any other. Before the horrible invasion by the Chinese in 1950, every Tibetan family donated their first son to the temple to become a monk for life, such is the connection between everyday life and the world beyond this one, and one would think that this constant search for closeness to the "beyond" has to result in some evidence. But, even the Tibetans could be wrong, especially when all religions try to "dumb down" their findings. **Eventually, they all create Easter Bunnies and Santa Clauses, because there simply are more people who cannot comprehend the truth than there are people who can.** Even Jesus Christ had secret teachings for just His disciples, teachings that were not to be shared with the common folk. You will have to ask the Creator Force why that discrepancy among us, but we are most certainly NOT created equal. That diversity among the Creation must be for a reason, but that reason is still being researched. The Tibetans believe that there is a sort of pyramid of life, that most beings begin at the bottom of the life cycle, and through successive reincarnations, they move up to higher planes of existence, finally leaving this life plane to move onto the next level of reincarnation, reincarnation after reincarnation, each life moving one's soul ever-upward, even in the life beyond this plane of existence, all of which leads ultimately to reuniting as one with the Great Creator of all of this. An example, you see a man lying in the gutter, a total drunk, having never achieved anything and obviously at the end of his life. How is he different from a nuclear physicist who has a wonderful life in a greatly rewarding job at a major university? Ponder it long, but the reality is that they will both die, but each will have a different ending to his life, an ending that is quantitative. And by quantitative, I do not mean how much money was in the bank account, but, rather, what peace was in their hearts. **One reincarnation tenet teaches that, at the moment of death, all that you are, everything about you, your passions, your hatreds, your loves, all of that is the seed for your next life.**

The Apostle John had the vision of the New Jerusalem, but he died without having ever seen that happen. The Apostle Paul preached about the end of times being in his day, and he went to his death without ever having witnessed that event. I am fully aware of those who say that the Bible does not even give these two apostles the right to predict the end, and that the end will come when it will come. And preachers have been calling their own day and time the end of days ever since Jesus Christ left, yet here we still are with preachers calling this the end of days, the end of time. And we have their defenders saying that scoffers will come in the "end of days" wondering why the end has been preached about, but has not happened. This classic rebuttal is designed to shut down all dissent, as if wondering why the "Rapture" has not happened in all of these centuries is a thought worthy only of apostates. That guilt trigger stops most Christians from having an original and investigative thought. But there is nothing wrong with asking why time has not come to an end, why Jesus has not come back to Earth, why John's vision in Revelation has never been realized on this planet. This is a healthy question for believers and non-believers alike. Why would the Apostle Paul choose death by beheading rather than change his beliefs? That set the gold standard for many Christians to come, even if the ideology of Heaven changed over time, and **we tend to hold on to all religious teachings as fact, because that is what we were taught. But what do we feel?**

In Luke 23:43, we read these words: "καὶ εἶπεν αὐτῷ Ἀμήν σοι λέγω, σήμερον μετ' ἐμοῦ ἔσῃ ἐν τῷ Παραδείσῳ." (Kai eipen auto Ameyn soi lego, seymeron met' emou esey en to Paradeiso.) Translating, "And He said to him, Truly, this day, thou shalt be with me in Paradise." The word used here in the Greek is "Παραδείσῳ" - "Paradeiso," "Paradise." Now, most Christians just think that Jesus was saying Heaven, but He said Paradise. At the time of Jesus, the concept of Paradise, as held by Jews, was a location in Hades, the abode of the dead, and this particular section of Hades was reserved for the righteous souls until the resurrection. Even the word "Paradise" was invented by the Persians and borrowed by the Jews, eventually making it into the Christian system of beliefs. The word Paradise does not exist in the original Hebrew description of the Garden of Eden. Here is Genesis 2:8 in Hebrew:

וַיִּטַּע יְהוָה אֱלֹהִים גַּן־בְעֵדֶן מִקֶּדֶם וַיָּשֶׂם שָׁם אֶת־הָאָדָם אֲשֶׁר יָצָר׃

Vayita Adonai Elohim gan-beden miqedem vayasem sam et-haadam asher yatsar.

Hebrew, by the way, is read from right to left. My English pronunciation guide is read left to right. The word for "Garden" here is גַּן "Gan." Later, as an example of the evolution of the word for garden, or park, in Nehemiah 2:8, we see the word for the king's "forest" rendered in Hebrew as "hapardes," הפרדס with "Pardes," meaning a garden, or park, with the same meaning as "gan." Centuries later, the translators of the Septuagint follow the Persians and change Eden from "gan," "garden," to "Paradaiso," "Paradise." As stated earlier, the Jewish concept of Paradise, even as early as the 3rd Century before Christ, was one of a repose after death for the righteous. However, as the Early Church began to form, and even as Christ ministered on Earth, the concept of the abode of the dead, the afterlife, was evolving even faster. Christ tells the thief in Luke 23:43, "Truly I tell you, today you will be with me in paradise." The Apostle John writes, in Revelation 2:7: "Whoever has ears, let them hear what the Spirit says to the churches. To the one who is victorious, I will give the right to eat from the tree of life, which is in the paradise of God." But we see variations on the theme with this passage in 2 Corinthians 5:1 "For we know that if the earthly tent we live in is destroyed, we have a building from God, an eternal house in heaven, not built by human hands." Here, Paul uses the words "... in heaven," "ἐν τοῖς οὐρανοῖς" (actually, "in the heavens") en tois ouranois. Now, where is Paul going with his placement of the "abode of the dead?"

Note, as well, how this evolution in Christianity continues to place the abode of the dead, the departed souls of the righteous, in "Heaven, a city prepared by God." Hebrews 11:13-16 "All these people were still living by faith when they died. They did not receive the things promised; they only saw them and welcomed them from a distance, admitting that they were foreigners and strangers on earth. People who say such things show that they are looking for a country of their own. If they had been thinking of the country they had left, they would have had opportunity to return. Instead, they were longing for a better country - a heavenly one. Therefore God is not ashamed to be called their God, for he has prepared a city for them."

Now, we can debate all day what and where Paradise is, when the concept began, and what it has come to mean, but Jesus on the cross simply told the thief who was being crucified with Him that the thief's soul would continue on to another plane of existence, a plane of existence that was superior to this one. Christians of today generally teach that Jesus was referring to Heaven, but He simply said... Paradise. And for purists, this would be in keeping with the prevailing beliefs of the Jews of the time of Jesus, the place in Hades reserved for the righteous dead awaiting the resurrection. **Interestingly enough, centuries after Jesus, the Early Church taught that Paradise was the origin of our first ancestors, a place where they dwelt before the Great Fall. They taught that this Paradise still exists, but that it was neither in the heavens, nor on the Earth. Paradise, the original home of the soul, was in a world beyond all of what we see.** Now THAT is interesting!

This concept of "Paradise" actually meshes with the study of death and the accounts of those who have been to the "Other Side" and back. What they see and report **is not a vision of a city, but a plane of existence that could very well be in a parallel universe,** since those who have experienced these Near-Death, or Out-Of-Body, events find themselves instantly there and often able to see back into this plane of Earth while being invisible to those here on Earth. In his book, Life After Life, Dr. Raymond Moody spent many years clinically investigating the stories of thousands of patients who had been pronounced dead and who had returned to tell what they had experienced while dead. A fascinating clinical study, the book shows the parallels each person had when out of their bodies, the meetings with dead relatives and loved ones in another plane of existence, as well, in many instances, of seeing "God." Dr. Moody stated: *"I don't mind saying that after talking with over a thousand people who have had these experiences, and having experienced many times some of the really baffling and unusual features of these experiences, it has given me great confidence that there is a life after death. As a matter of fact, I must confess to you in all honesty, I have absolutely no doubt, on the basis of what my patients have told me, that they did get a glimpse of the beyond."*

A vast array of religions have come and gone, down through the ages, and this current world is equally filled with a comparative array, each with their beliefs on what we experience once we leave this human body. Much of the universe does not make philosophically logical sense when one starts to ask too many questions. Such questions as "Why are we here on Earth as opposed to elsewhere?" - "Why do we exist?" - "Why is this world filled with war and pain?" - "Why doesn't God just tell us the answers to everything?" and countless others come to mind, questions that often make simple faith either easy or difficult. There are three ways to look at it all. The simplistic, **Fundamentalist Method** is total belief in a set of taught ideals, never questioning, always accepting, and using that core of beliefs to bring peace and happiness to a life lived to the end. The fatalist **Resigned Method** is to have questions nagging at the brain, but to simply suppress them with a thought that it will all work its way out in the end, and to tell oneself that we cannot know anything for sure. These people either follow a religious ideal blindly hoping that it is true, or they become atheists who hide their fears in a locked closet. And there is the **Reality Method** for those who have minds that have been freed from fear and who are willing to explore in their search for God and Truth. **For all three groups, death will come equally and without bias, the Afterlife will come as constructed by the Creator Force, even if we, with our finite minds, cannot reason the equation with satisfaction.** Heaven, after all, may be just a "waiting area" where, as the Tibetans teach, we plan our return in another life here on this plane of existence, or we move up a ladder of successive incarnations to finally merge with the Spirit of our Great Creator. And for whatever purpose the Creator Force made all of us, made all of the confusing and conflicting history that we have recorded, both horrific and peaceful, both fearful and heart-warming, both despicable and inspiring, the bad and the good all have their source in the Creator Force who allowed it all to happen, and, thus, for reasons known only to the Creator Force, ordained its passage in time. The Creator Force is the author of all that has ever been, all that is and all that ever will be. When we have ended our lives, we are instantly transported to the next "station" in the plans of the Creator Force. But, there the mystery deepens. Once "there," do we await a return to this plane of existence for some "educational" experience, as is taught by the believers in reincarnation? Do we stay on the other side in the realm of the Afterlife never to go anywhere else? Does the Creator Force have another set of plans that will begin another "play" similar to the one written by the history of this planet? Is there another Creation set somewhere in the far distant future? Did the prophet Isaiah get it right when he said in the book of Isaiah 65:17

"See, I will create new heavens and a new earth. The former things will not be remembered, nor will they come to mind."

The Creator Force made all that is, ever has been and ever will be, which includes every living creature on this planet. I cannot speak for the Creator Force, nor can I speak for the plans of the Creator Force regarding what awaits us in eternity, but I do know that what I experienced when I was taken out of my body and into the presence of the Creator Force, the dead loved ones with whom I spoke while there, all point to one thing that I <u>DO</u> know about the Afterlife; call it what you will, but we leave this plane of existence, without ever losing consciousness, and we are immediately in a plane of existence that operates on a totally different set of physics principles. Believe what you will until you get there, call it whatever name makes you comfortable, but there is most definitely something waiting for all of us. In the dying experience of the famous computer genius, Steve Jobs, just as he expired and his physical eyes gave way to the eyes of those who are transitioning to the Afterlife, he uttered just one word - "Wow!" Think on that. Now that he was leaving behind the physics of this world, no longer bound by our limitations, at that tiny moment between worlds, what did he see?

Where Am I Going When I Leave Here? - Part Two

Painting, circa 1900, depicting saints, at the top, being welcomed into the New Jerusalem by Jesus Christ, while sinners, at bottom, are welcomed into the gates of Hell.

    Most people who practice Christianity, whether they know it or not, get their ideas of what Heaven is from the Book of Revelation. Here, from the King James Version (KJV), we read the origins of the description that has prevailed:

21 "And I saw a new heaven and a new earth: for the first heaven and the first earth were passed away; and there was no more sea.

² And I John saw the holy city, new Jerusalem, coming down from God out of heaven, prepared as a bride adorned for her husband.

³ And I heard a great voice out of heaven saying, Behold, the tabernacle of God is with men, and he will dwell with them, and they shall be his people, and God himself shall be with them, and be their God.

⁴ And God shall wipe away all tears from their eyes; and there shall be no more death, neither sorrow, nor crying, neither shall there be any more pain: for the former things are passed away.

⁵ And he that sat upon the throne said, Behold, I make all things new. And he said unto me, Write: for these words are true and faithful.

⁶ And he said unto me, It is done. I am Alpha and Omega, the beginning and the end. I will give unto him that is athirst of the fountain of the water of life freely.

⁷ He that overcometh shall inherit all things; and I will be his God, and he shall be my son.

⁸ But the fearful, and unbelieving, and the abominable, and murderers, and whoremongers, and sorcerers, and idolaters, and all liars, shall have their part in the lake which burneth with fire and brimstone: which is the second death.

⁹ And there came unto me one of the seven angels which had the seven vials full of the seven last plagues, and talked with me, saying, Come hither, I will shew thee the bride, the Lamb's wife.

¹⁰ And he carried me away in the spirit to a great and high mountain, and shewed me that great city, the holy Jerusalem, descending out of heaven from God,

¹¹ Having the glory of God: and her light was like unto a stone most precious, even like a jasper stone, clear as crystal;

¹² And had a wall great and high, and had twelve gates, and at the gates twelve angels, and names written thereon, which are the names of the twelve tribes of the children of Israel:

¹³ On the east three gates; on the north three gates; on the south three gates; and on the west three gates.

¹⁴ And the wall of the city had twelve foundations, and in them the names of the twelve apostles of the Lamb.

¹⁵ And he that talked with me had a golden reed to measure the city, and the gates thereof, and the wall thereof.

¹⁶ And the city lieth foursquare, and the length is as large as the breadth: and he measured the city with the reed, twelve thousand furlongs. The length and the breadth and the height of it are equal.

¹⁷ And he measured the wall thereof, an hundred and forty and four cubits, according to the measure of a man, that is, of the angel.

¹⁸ And the building of the wall of it was of jasper: and the city was pure gold, like unto clear glass.

¹⁹ And the foundations of the wall of the city were garnished with all manner of precious stones. The first foundation was jasper; the second, sapphire; the third, a chalcedony; the fourth, an emerald;

²⁰ The fifth, sardonyx; the sixth, sardius; the seventh, chrysolyte; the eighth, beryl; the ninth, a topaz; the tenth, a chrysoprasus; the eleventh, a jacinth; the twelfth, an amethyst.

²¹ And the twelve gates were twelve pearls: every several gate was of one pearl: and the street of the city was pure gold, as it were transparent glass.

²² And I saw no temple therein: for the Lord God Almighty and the Lamb are the temple of it.

²³ And the city had no need of the sun, neither of the moon, to shine in it: for the glory of God did lighten it, and the Lamb is the light thereof.

²⁴ And the nations of them which are saved shall walk in the light of it: and the kings of the earth do bring their glory and honour into it.

²⁵ And the gates of it shall not be shut at all by day: for there shall be no night there.

²⁶ And they shall bring the glory and honour of the nations into it.

²⁷ And there shall in no wise enter into it any thing that defileth, neither whatsoever worketh abomination, or maketh a lie: but they which are written in the Lamb's book of life."

With these written words of John in the Book of Revelation, a new ideology of what Heaven was going to be for believers began to take hold and evolve throughout the Early Church, and eventually, throughout the known world. Perhaps by this passage from the Book of Revelation more than any other, the ideas of "what Heaven is" have been colored. I am often asked about what Heaven is, as well as where Heaven is, especially because of the experience I had at age fifteen when I was taken out of my body and into the presence of the Creator Force.

To share that experience, here is what happened to me. From before I could remember, my father was a preacher in the Church of God, which was, at that time, a very strict sect of Fundamentalist churches, and my family's life revolved around the church. Our religion, as I once angrily told me father, was a lot of "don'ts." We were not allowed to go to public beaches, we could not wear shorts in public, we were not permitted to dance, women could not cut their hair nor could they wear makeup of any kind, we were not permitted to wear any kind of jewelry (eventually they gave in to allowing a plain wedding ring for married couples), could not play cards, touch dice, go to movies, go bowling, listen to "worldly" music, and the list went on. It was a lot of "you can't do this, and you can't do that," but I was born and raised in it, so that was all I knew. I saw the world as "them," and "we," the Pentecostals, were God's people. We lived separate lives from "them."

Church was Sunday morning for two to three hours, Sunday night for two to three hours, and we had a mid-week church service called the Wednesday night prayer meeting, which was several hours long, as well. We were fervent in our worship, and if the Spirit moved, we could be there for five or six hours, so Pentecostal services were lengthy and high-spirited. That was our regular church schedule, and even though we came home from church on most Sundays before going back for the evening service, we made the entire day a "holy" day, which meant absolutely no work, and usually meant visiting members of the congregation during the afternoon before going back to church. Now, as if that was not enough church time, if we were holding revival, church services would be every night for a week, sometimes two weeks, if the church wanted to keep it going. Thus, our lives truly revolved around the church. We felt that the Rapture was going to take place in our time, an event that Pentecostals believe means the moment Jesus Christ returns to Earth to take all of His "saved" righteous Christians to the new kingdom with Him. So, we lived in fear of missing that event, and that fear kept us going to church. Funny how that cycle works. It is still used today.

Pentecostal women were not permitted to cut their hair, so they created artful ways to braid and curl it on top of their heads when they wanted it out of the way. This may have been the source of the Bee Hive hairdo that became popular later in the Sixties.

The Pentecostal churches in that day were very much into what was called "charismatic events." What this means is that they firmly believed that the origins of their faith began on the Day of Pentecost described in the book of Acts, wherein the apostles were waiting in the famous "Upper Room" for the "Comforter" to come, the "Comforter" being the Spirit of God, or, as they liked to call it, the Holy Ghost. Pentecostals in that era believed that, if you prayed long enough, and had purified your life by "getting saved," a process whereby you prayed for forgiveness from Jesus Christ for your "sins," accepted Jesus as your "Savior," you were ready to be imbued with this permanent visitation of the Holy Ghost. You would be praying, asking God to "baptize you with the Holy Ghost," and when God was ready, be it minutes of praying, hours of praying, or even days, months or years, when it finally came, you would experience the indescribable phenomenon of being "baptized with the Holy Ghost." When this event would happen, the seeker would suddenly become rapturous, euphoric, and go into a trance state where they might stay for minutes or hours, but it was pure ecstatic joy for the recipient. And the sign that it was of God was that the person who was now baptized in the Holy Ghost would begin to "speak in tongues." This portion of the experience was believed by Pentecostals to be the exact same experience had by the apostles and the Early Church on the Day of Pentecost in Jerusalem around A.D. 33. Thus, it was inevitable that I would be taught that, once I was "saved," I should want to progress to seeking this experience for myself.

It was 1966, during a revival service at our little Church of God in Oxford, Pennsylvania, and I was fifteen years old. I had become a zealot for all things taught by the Church of God, thinking that everything that I was taught was straight from God. After all, didn't god speak to us from the pulpit? In the Fundamentalist churches, a revival would be a week of nightly church services, and we Pentecostals knew how to have a long church service. 7 p.m. to 9 p.m. was a routine service, and it would begin with prayer, then music worship, congregational hymns and special singers, then an offering, more music, some testimonies (where people stood up an exhorted the church by relating religious blessings that they had recently experienced), congregational prayer where everyone came and knelt at the altar up in front of the pulpit, and when it was finally time, the preaching would start. A routine sermon was thirty minutes, but a good one could go on for hours. I have literally sat and listened to a preacher go on for four hours once. At the end of the sermon, there would be an altar call, as they termed it, during which the preacher would ask people to come to the altar and pray. This would be when some people came up to get saved, and others came up for prayer for healing. It was also a time for those seeking the Holy Ghost to continue that pursuit. After all, what better time to pray for this exciting experience than when the music was going, and so many people were up there praying with you and for you. So, there I was, kneeling in front of that altar that was nothing more than a row of hard-back chairs arranged in a row. I prayed for an hour three nights in a row, and it was on that third night that something happened. As I was praying, I saw a vision of Jesus Christ on the cross. There was so much turmoil around him, Roman soldiers, people screaming and yelling, and as I looked up at Him in sorrow at what I was beholding, He smiled at me and told me not to worry, that He would be okay. Then, He told me to keep walking forward. It was at that moment, doing as He bade me, that I suddenly found myself in what I instantly knew was Heaven. I was surrounded by a white mist, and the things of this world disappeared completely. I no longer heard anything from inside the church. I was completely oblivious to anything that was still going on there, completely removed from it. I had left my body.

The first thing I saw was four people emerging from the mist, and I instantly recognized them. My aunt Barbara Ann, her mother (and my grandmother), Oresa Mercer, an elderly lady from our church whom we called Mother Harris, and her daughter whom we had always called Sister Harris. Barbara Ann had been mentally retarded, so much so that she was like a child in an adult body. I always remembered her as a playful kid. She died, sadly, in an institution when she was 28 years old. Her mother, my grandmother Oresa

Mercer, had died from high blood pressure just before Barbara Ann's untimely death. My grandmother was 47 years old when she passed; fell over in church and was gone forever. Mother Harris died of old age and a broken heart, I think, because her daughter, Sister Harris, was killed while driving through an intersection. And these were the four people who came to greet me.

I was so excited to see them, filled with tremendous joy, and intriguingly enough, I went down the row and hugged each of them. Then I repeated that entire greeting once again. Why twice? I think because of the awe and joy of just being there with them. Then, I looked at Barbara Ann. We were smiling at each other, just beaming with joy, and I was still in such shock and awe, that I began to speak. But I had said no more than the first three words when I heard Barbara Ann's voice in my head, all while she was just standing in front of me, beaming with that radiant smile and glow about her. She said, "You don't have to speak here." In other words, everything was telepathic. And mid-sentence, I switched from trying to speak with my mouth and just finished the sentence with my mind. Sure enough, we were conversing at light speed, and it was all between our minds. I was fascinated by this ability. However, most amazing to me at that point was the fact that I had always remembered Barbara Ann as severely retarded, but here, when she looked into my eyes, the sensation was seeing limitless wisdom and knowledge, that she knew more about the universe than all of Earth's scientists put together. Her eyes literally could see all the way down into my soul. I was stunned into silence and just stared into them, absolutely stunned!

At some point, I turned to my right, and there was an intense light off in the near distance. I knew immediately and without question who this was—Almighty God! The Being was not a man, not a woman, but a nearly indescribable light that was brighter than the sun. That "Presence" dominated the area, and the closer I looked toward the central focal point of it, the more intense and impenetrable and dense was this powerful light. Strangely enough, I was able to look right at this light without being blinded. I stood there in awe, overwhelmed by the majesty of this being. I sensed the extreme intelligence, which is an understatement. This being knew everything there was to know, and I instantly knew that everything that has ever been, everything that is, and everything that ever will be, emanated from this source. This was the Creator Force that so many called simply God. And as I stood there, I saw that the light, like a beautiful, fiery white mist that swirled like it was alive, because it was alive, very much so, had moved toward me and was approaching rapidly like a giant tidal wave filling all the space around me. I knew that I was about to be engulfed by this light, and I knew it was my God. I felt unworthy. I had been taught that there were so many things that I did that were "sins," things for which I had never prayed for forgiveness, little things in the past, but, nonetheless, they were "impurities" that I felt were going to stand out like black spots on a cancer x-ray image. I just knew that, when God completely engulfed me with His presence, He was going to immediately recoil and say something to the effect that I needed to cleanse myself spiritually before I was to be permitted to be that close to Him. I just knew that, as soon as that light touched me, it was going to recoil, to race away from me... but, it didn't!

While I stood there, frozen with thoughts of how unworthy I was, I was completely engulfed by the presence of God. Surrounded, permeated, through and through, there was not one atom of my body that was not completely saturated with the presence of this Light. And instead of being condemned, like some sinner in a Fundamentalist church service who was told how sinful they were and how in need of change they were, all I felt, **ALL I felt, was indescribable LOVE!** I was loved! Through and through, every atom in my body was feeling the greatest and most indescribable love, a love that this world cannot even come close to duplicating. From that moment forward, and to this day, I have felt a constant connection to this Force, my God, the Creator Force. I still have no fear of death, because I know, like the biblical passage that refers to "being absent from the body is to be present with the Lord," I believe that when I leave this physical "suit" behind, I simply walk back into that realm, the realm, I am convinced, from which I came.

In a short moment of time later, while still in this mist of light, I saw my deceased grandmother, Oresa Mercer, standing there. And this part is almost funny. I looked at her and pleadingly asked if there was someone that she or I could talk to about staying there and not returning to Earth. I remember her words to this day, "It is not your time. You have things to do yet on Earth. But, you will be back." I was saddened and disappointed at the resolve in her voice when she stated that I could not stay. I felt an almost frantic need to change her mind, yet my religious beliefs kept me from expressing it further, as if I would be morally wrong, somehow, to ask again. Equally, that resolve in her voice and face told me everything. It would be useless to ask again. Still, I was somewhat heartened by her promise that I would be coming back there at some time in the future. At that very moment, I saw what appeared to me as an angel coming from within the white mist of light and to my right. Whether the angel was male or female, I could not tell you, but the angel was like I would have drawn in some portrait, except there were no wings. The angel had a face, but I dared not stare out of pure religious reverence wrought from my strict upbringing. I was unworthy, but I saw enough of the angel to see that there was a face, while the body was wrapped in white light, like the angel was wearing a robe that flowed about the body. The gentle, yet authoritative, voice came into my mind, "Follow me." I knew that I was being led away from this paradise, and it saddened and disappointed me. I dutifully turned to follow the angel, and, very quickly, there in front of me was what appeared to be a stone wall with an arched opening, a doorway, and on the other side of this doorway, I could see outer space. Black, with stars dotting the emptiness, and there in the distance was the planet Earth floating in this sea of space. It was brilliant blue and white, just like photos from space would show it. At this very moment, the angel said, "Walk forward."

I looked at the surface whereon we stood, and from the arched doorway outward, there were what appeared to be cobblestones. However, as the cobblestones continued outward from where we were standing, they rapidly became spaced further and further apart, until, with just a few feet, there was absolutely nothing but the deep darkness of outer space punctuated with stars off in the distance. I momentarily felt a pang of fear. In that brief moment, I had peered down over the edge of this rather short pier, the end of those cobblestones abrupt before me. I could literally look down through the spaces in those stones and see the vast emptiness of space below, and this angel had just told me to walk forward. "Does this angel know that I can't fly?" I thought to myself. I looked alarmedly at the increasing spaces between those stones. There was rapid thought going through my brain. What do I do? I am going to fall to my death. Should I ask this angel how I am supposed to do this? But, I thought, asking that question would be challenging God. I had been raised on the many meanings of the word "faith." In my religion, faith meant no questioning. Instantly, I had resolved that, if I were to fall into this vastness and eventually die, I would be resurrected by God. If I had to die this way in order to come back here, I was resigned to all of this. I stepped forward. One foot went forward, the second foot went forward, and I was just in the middle of raising my next foot for the third step when... I was lying on my back in front of the altar in the church service. I was lying there, sprawled out on the floor and "speaking in tongues," a phenomenon I will discuss some other time, but the euphoria was real, and the experience was valid, something that would stay with me for the rest of my life. It is for this reason that I will never deny the existence of the Creator Force, or God, as some like to call this being, and I will never deny the existence of this abode of our souls after we leave this plane of existence. It was real, very real, tangibly real, and for those who like to debunk this by saying that it was just a chemical reaction in my brain, I appreciate where you are coming from. My brain could never invent the physics of this reality. Furthermore, if this had been a creation of my brain, I would have seen my aunt, Barbara Ann, as still severely retarded. I would have had no other construct from which to draw, and she would have been painted just the way I remembered her. My brain would have had no other reference point. She was, instead, wiser and more intelligent than I can describe. She had the wisdom of the ages in her eyes, she was changed, and not by my imagination, but by the reality of a world I could not have created. The world beyond here is real!

Suffice it to say, because of what I experienced, I have a different view of the afterlife than most people, and because of my education among various world religions and world philosophies, I do not share the standard view of what Heaven actually is. Explaining Heaven is far more complicated than the average mind can begin to comprehend, but I still think it is wise to explore the subject. After all, everyone born on this planet is destined to leave this plane of existence sooner or later, and ignoring what comes after this existence will not change destiny.

In the Book of Revelation, John describes a new Heaven and Earth, and he sees a city that is a new Jerusalem that is brought down to this planet, a city with streets of pure gold and a construction that is dazzling to say the least. Whatever we are to make of this vision of John, there are several things to remember here: in John's world, Jerusalem would be akin to Washington, D.C. Jerusalem was a power center, both politically and religiously, so what better focal point for a new beginning for this planet? At least in the world of the apostles, this idea would have resonated as highly probable. To believers, this is a sacred vision, while to atheists, John was hallucinating, nothing more, nothing less. After all, they will point out, the Apostle Paul wrote often about the "end of time," and Paul expected that to take place in his lifetime. In Paul's idea and John's vision of the New Kingdom, suppression excesses of the Roman Empire would be done away with, and in the place of corrupt human emperors, God, Himself, would rule with supreme justice... right here on Earth. The center of political and religious life, this new Jerusalem, would become the center of the universe, and the early apostles would have very important places of respect in this new order. It is easy to draw conclusions about the desires of the oppressed, those who suffered greatly under Roman occupation. Longing to be released from the centuries of brutal Roman rule was a desire passed down from generation to generation. Thus, a new Heaven and Earth had to come, and with it a new Jerusalem, a Jerusalem so perfect that even the very streets were paved with gold that was so pure, it was translucent. In fact, John's vision had the entire city made of this translucent gold. Since that vision of John's so many centuries ago, John, who had the vision, and Paul, who truly expected to see the new kingdom in his lifetime, both have long since passed into history, never having seen their beliefs come true. But the story of that visionary city with streets paved in gold did not die with Paul or John. To the contrary, that vision of the heavenly kingdom on Earth has evolved into a belief in a Heaven filled with the most luxurious of rewards for those who are believers. The concept of Heaven, the belief in Heaven, has been told and retold down through the centuries, and if you think that your idea of Heaven matches that of the Early Church, you are very wrong. Yet still, most Christians think that all Christians think alike on that subject, that all share the exact same picture of what and where Heaven is. But what is reality? Does the Heaven described by most Christians actually exist?

To answer that last question, let's dig deeper. For many Christians, it is easy to simply think that Heaven is some perfect and idyllic paradise that has been described to them since childhood. The idea sits somewhere in the back of their heads. Pressed for details, a strange look comes over their faces, and they excuse their lack of detail by saying that the exact details will all just sort themselves out after death. Faith... you simply believe it is so... and it is. Simplistic? Yes, and yet, this may be all that most people need to get through life. If one's life span was five years, dying as a child, don't you think it would be convenient to simply allow the child to have a story that brought calm, as opposed to one that brought apprehension? When we are children, adults tell us about Santa Claus, about tooth fairies, even the Easter Bunny, and these elaborate tales keep us happy as children. The stories seem to make sense to a young mind, and after all, they are told to us by those older and wiser than ourselves. Why question? We children simply believe... and it is so. At what point do these same adults tell these happy children that life is a bit more complicated? That life is not as simple as they made it out to be? And what changes then? **Does the world change, or does a story change? The factual world is reality. What is real will always be real, regardless of how we paint over the window that looks into that reality. Regardless of the stories we tell each other to keep us happy and calm, none of our stories will change reality.** If there is no Santa Claus, then there never was one. But when it comes to our religious beliefs, beliefs that were handed down to us and taught to us with the utmost belief in their sanctity, at what point in our lives are we willing to pull back the curtain separating us from truth and peer into the "other room?" When do we desire to know the real answers to the questions, questions that we are taught have answers that can only be accepted by faith, not logic? Can we "know" the truth about Heaven?

The Concept of Heaven and Hell

Nothing motivates bad people to shape up and fly right like the reward and punishment concept of Heaven and Hell. This concept is nothing new, and it did not originate with the Christian religion. If you study world religions, both past and present, you will find a system where the dead are judged and rewarded according to their actions while in the land of the living. In the Dhammapada (147:51), Buddha is speaking of the decay of the body, an object in which we seem to put too much of life's emphasis, rather than on the good works of Dharma, or the path of right living.

"Behold this beautiful body, a mass of sores, a heaped up lump, diseased, much thought of, in which nothing lasts, nothing persists. Thoroughly worn out is this body, a nest of diseases, perishable.... Truly, life ends in death.... Of bones is this house made, plastered with flesh and blood. Herein are stored decay, death, conceit, and hypocrisy. Even ornamented royal chariots wear out. So too the body reaches old age. But the Dharma of the Good grows not old. Thus do the Good reveal it among the Good."

The Buddha, then, is exhorting people to live a life of contemplation, a life given to the study of the spiritual as opposed to the fleshly desires.

"Men who have not led a religious life and have not laid up treasure in their youth, perish like old herons in a lake without fish. Men who have not led a religious life and have not laid up treasure in their youth lie like worn out bows, sighing after the past." (Dhammapada 155:56)

Jesus Christ said the same thing in Matthew 6:19-21

"Do not lay up for yourselves treasures on earth, where moth and rust destroy and where thieves break in and steal, but lay up for yourselves treasures in heaven, where neither moth nor rust destroys and where thieves do not break in and steal. For where your treasure is, there will your heart be also."

There are basically two kinds of human beings: those who can understand the metaphysical, and those who cannot. I honestly believe that most religious tenets are for those in the latter category, those who will never be able to comprehend the need for spiritual living and, thus, need the "Heaven and Hell" sermons to get them focused on the life beyond this one. For many in the former category, there is a mental battle, one that revolves around letting go of the children's tales and exploring the realities that are there with regard to this life and the next. When you have been taught all your life that violating the teachings of your church is going to send you straight to Hell, even though your intelligence groans for answers that these children's stories do not satisfy, call it comfortable sentimentality, something that is familiar and easy to follow, or call it outright fear that maybe these people are actually right, but what you were taught will give you a real battle over accepting anything that differs from those teachings. So, let's just look at the one I was raised in, Christianity.

As I have mentioned before, you can ask any Christian what their idea of Heaven is and what their idea of Hell is, and even if you ask one thousand of them this question, you will get one thousand different descriptions. Why is that? Because no Christian church ever takes the time to really sit down and study this subject other than to quote a biblical passage that supports the concept so that they can artfully include it in a sermon. That's it! Period! Small wonder there is no consensus on what these two places actually look like and how they operate. Christians just know that they are there, somewhere off in the skies for Heaven, and somewhere "down below" for Hell. They will usually be able to tell you that you get a mansion in Heaven, and you burn forever in Hell with flames like you've never seen. But here's the shocking thing about their descriptions: the Bible does not give the same picture.

The concept of an afterlife reward for the righteous and the wicked is as varied as time and history itself. But the concepts of these two places are not inventions of the Christians. Every religion shares this much in common: after death, the person goes somewhere. That person may go as a soul, or as some other configuration of components, and the abode of that soul can either be bad or good, torturous and eternal, or torturous and temporary, good and eternal, or good and temporary. For example, you may go to Hell and be tortured for a short period, then, as the Babylonian Talmud says, "...after twelve months their bodies are destroyed, their souls are burned, and the wind strews the ashes under the feet of the pious." Or, as the Catholic Church invented in the 16th Century, you might go to a "limbo" where, after time and the intercession of good people, maybe even a little money, you are released and sent on to Heaven. But as we read ancient literature, we find that even these "rules" get bent for some people. For example, the same Babylonian Talmud says there is an exception for the heretics, and Jeroboam, Nebat's son. For them "... hell shall pass away, but they shall not pass away." **Interesting how such punishments are interchangeable and controlled by the gatekeepers... humans in charge of the temples.**

As I mentioned, ask any Christian where Heaven is, and they will point upward. This belief that Heaven is somewhere "up there," has not been around that long, and really began in the days of the Early Church. The afterlife for those of the Judaic tradition in the Old Testament was Sheol, the abode of the dead, and this concept really was not a parallel of the Greek concept of the afterlife... and don't forget who influenced the writings of the New Testament, the Greeks. The Greek word for the starry sky, the atmosphere, the visible heavens, or the spiritual heavens was οὐρανός, pronounced "oo-rahn-NOS." Thus, whenever you read the word Heaven, such as in "Heavenly kingdom," for example, in the English, the word in the original Greek is this same "Ouranos." Thus, Heaven is the place of the dead that was now being placed somewhere "up there in the skies." We human beings were evolving in our spiritual views. The abode of the dead was being taken out of the ground and placed somewhere a little more delightful than that dark dungeon underground. And never forget this, the abode of the dead was always changing as humans progressed in their understandings of the universe. The Bible is silent on a description of what is the composition of Heaven, in spite of those who misinterpret the vision of John the Revelator in his "New Jerusalem" as being Heaven. That was not Heaven. That was what John saw as the new government on Earth that was brought down from Ouranos, the heavens

Consider this, the early Christians put Heaven "out there" somewhere among the stars, and now we have the technology to send satellites racing past what the naked eye can see from Earth. So far, these satellites haven't bumped into anything that resembles the New Jerusalem, or anything resembling where our righteous elders have gathered. And all of this gives more credence to the idea that **the abode of the souls is not in this plane of existence. Give that abode any name that brings you comfort, but physical man cannot enter. The soul can, because that is not only the home of the soul, it is the origin of the soul.**

I can still remember the time I had just reached a point of mental stress that boiled over into my giving in to an exasperated moment and virtually whispering an epithet under my breath, or what I thought was under my breath, and some obese woman standing nearby with her young daughter apparently was able to hear my inappropriate use of the Lord's name. Literally gasping for breath, she turned to me, an indescribable look on her face, but something like sheer disgust and horror, and with red-faced venom, she shouted, "You're going to Hell! You're going to Hell!" You can figure the rest, but, at the time, I was not as devoted a Christian, so her remarks most certainly did not have the impact that she had hoped for (and I doubt that they would have any better impact on me today, for that matter). Nonetheless, her reaction and use of the word "Hell" actually represents the extreme lack of understanding of what Hell actually means, both in a religious sense and a literal sense. Most people have their own theological ideas of just what Hell is... as well as where Hell is. Ask 1,000 people what they know about Hell, and you will get 1,000 different stories. **Here is some food for thought... much religious ideology is based on hearsay.**

People will go running to their Bibles to quote verse after verse to explain their belief that Hell is the hottest place in the universe, that it is right under our feet, and that solely because the word appears in their Bible, Hell is real... and their idea of exactly what Hell is, well, then that is exactly what Hell is... to Hell with anybody else's ideas. And these individual ideas of Hell have been handed down from region to region, from people to people, from religious group to religious group without anyone ever stopping to say, "Wait, let's explore this a bit." When Christians go running to the Bible for their favorite "proofs," the first problem encountered is their complete dependence on the English word in front of them. Let's look, for example, at the first time in the New Testament where the word Hell appears:

Matthew 5:22 "But anyone who says, 'You fool,' will be in danger of the fire of hell." There you have it, the word Hell appears in the Bible, case closed. The typical Fundamentalist will be able to quote a number of scriptural locations all using the word Hell, or lake of fire, or abyss, or any of several other metaphors used to refer to this seeming absolute. Let's take a look at that verse of Matthew 5:22 in the original Greek:

ἐγὼ δὲ λέγω ὑμῖν ὅτι πᾶς ὁ ὀργιζόμενος τῷ ἀδελφῷ αὐτοῦ ἔνοχος ἔσται τῇ κρίσει· ὃς δ' ἂν εἴπῃ τῷ ἀδελφῷ αὐτοῦ Ῥακά, ἔνοχος ἔσται τῷ συνεδρίῳ· ὃς δ' ἂν εἴπῃ Μωρέ, ἔνοχος ἔσται εἰς τὴν γέενναν τοῦ πυρός.

So, for calling your brother a Μωρέ (pronounced—Moe reh), a fool, you are doomed to this horrible place, Hell? The word for Hell here (third word from the end of the sentence) is γέενναν (pronounced geennan), and the phrase "fire of hell," in the original Greek is τὴν γέενναν τοῦ πυρός, (pronounced - teyn geennan tou puros, "puros" meaning "fire"). So what is the "fire of geennan"? In virtually every passage in the New Testament that uses the word Hell, the word is always the same... geennan. Of course, there are several times when the afterlife of the "damned" is described using other words, such as :

Luke 16:23 "In hell, where he was in torment, he looked up and saw Abraham, who was far away, with Lazarus by his side." Here is the original Greek:

καὶ ἐν τῷ ᾅδῃ ἐπάρας τοὺς ὀφθαλμοὺς αὐτοῦ, ὑπάρχων ἐν βασάνοις, ὁρᾷ Ἀβραὰμ ἀπὸ μακρόθεν καὶ Λάζαρον ἐν τοῖς κόλποις αὐτοῦ.

Note the fourth word in this Greek phrase - καὶ ἐν τῷ ᾅδῃ (pronounced - kai en toe hahdey). ᾅδῃ (pronounced hahdey) means Hades! The four Greek words at the beginning of this sentence translate as, "And in Hades...." So, this sentence in the original Greek actually reads, "In Hades, where he was in torment..." Borrowing from Greek mythology, this word, Hades, the mythological abode of the dead, is here used in the Bible. Why? I will come to that, but first, here is another reference to the abode of the damned:

2 Peter 2:4 "For if God spared not the angels that sinned, but cast them down to hell, and delivered them into chains of darkness, to be reserved unto judgment;" Here is the original Greek:

εἰ γὰρ ὁ Θεὸς ἀγγέλων ἁμαρτησάντων οὐκ ἐφείσατο, ἀλλὰ σειροῖς ζόφου ταρταρώσας παρέδωκεν εἰς κρίσιν τηρουμένους,

Here, in the original Greek, the word geennan, does not appear. Instead, we now have ταρταρώσας (pronounced - tartarosas). This is the same Tartaros, or Tartarus, of ancient Greek mythology, the deep abyss that was used as a dungeon of torment for the wicked and the prison of the Titans (more on this prison in a moment). The other word we see here is ζόφου (pronounced zophou) meaning "of gloomy darkness." The phrase is: σειροῖς ζόφου ταρταρώσας (pronounced - seyrois zophou tartarosas) and means, "in chains of gloomy darkness having cast them to the deepest abyss (Tartaros)." What are these terms, and to what do they refer? Let's look now at the mythology of Hades.

The place of the Underworld was named after its ruler, Hades, the brother of Zeus and Poseidon, gods of Mt. Olympus. When these three brothers overthrew their father, Cronus, they drew lots to see who would rule which sectors of the universe, and Hades drew the lot of Lord of the Underworld. Hades had a three-headed dog named Cerberus that helped guard his realm. The journey to the Underworld realm of Hades involved being ferried across the river Styx by the ferryman, Charon, although earlier Greek versions tell that the river was Acheron. When the three brothers, Hades, Zeus and Poseidon, overthrew their father, they drove the Titan gods into a pit beneath Hades called Tartaros and locked them away therein. When souls arrived at the shores of Hades, they were met by three judges, Minos, Rhadamanthys and Aiakos. Souls that were judged as having lived good lives were taken to drink of the waters of the River Lethe, which would make them forget all bad things, and then they were taken to the Elysian Fields to live forever in idyllic conditions. Those souls judged to have lived bad lives were given

Hades and his three-headed dog, Cerberus

into the hands of the Furies, taken to Tartaros, and there tortured. Finally, those who offended the gods were sentenced to eternal torment. This mythical ideology plays heavily into the Early Christian concepts of Hell.

Knowing this bit of Greek mythology, revisit the verse in 2 Peter 2:4, and remember that Peter was a Greek. Here, he writes that God cast the angels into the darkness of Tartaros. Most Sunday School classes are never going to discuss this, and that is primarily because most Sunday School classes are not taught by anyone with sufficient education in the Greek classics to get the connection. This is serious information to analyze, because what we see in 2 Peter 2:4 is a direct use of the mythology of Hades and Tartaros. The only difference here is that instead of the three Titan gods sending the other Titan gods into Tartaros, it is the Christian God sending some of His angels there. Yet, ask any Christian where Tartaros is, and they would venture a guess, at best, that it was some ancient city in the Roman Empire. Tell them that it is a place connected to the Greek mythological underworld of Hades, and they would most likely laugh and say, "Well, we don't believe in Greek mythology in our religion." However, without studying their Bible and Greek mythology, especially the original language and culture of the New Testament, I'm afraid these corollary facts are lost on them, and the whole idea of Hell just keeps getting re-colored and re-colored with each passing generation to serve whatever need the idea of Hell serves.

One more point to note here is that in the Old Testament, whenever the Greek translations insert geennan, the word is actually Sheol, the Jewish concept of the abode of the dead, and these two words are not the same. In ancient Judaic culture, the thinking about the afterlife was that souls went on a one-way trip to the center of the planet Earth. One way that Sheol differs from Hell is that Sheol was not a place of punishment, even though Sheol was divided into two compartments - one for the righteous and one for the wicked. Why Sheol was thought of as literally beneath the Earth may have been from an extension of the thoughts surrounding human burials. Whatever the reason for this religious view, modern science was not around back then to show these ancients that the Earth can be understood all the way to its very core, and there is no room for some huge repository of dead souls, especially when the descriptions of Sheol give it a paradise-like quality complete with parallels to the land of the living. Furthermore, descriptions of Sheol continued to evolve over the centuries that passed from the time of its inception when first handed down from the Assyrians, but Sheol and Hades are not the same place, and they do not share any other similarities other than an abode of the dead. Thus, when one reads an Old Testament passage and comes across the word Hell in English, the word Hell has been substituted for Sheol, and the New Testament uses the word Hades, a very important fact to keep in mind when studying the ideology of Hell.

If one reads 1 Samuel 28:6-20, there is the story of King Saul requesting the witch of Endor to bring up the spirit of the prophet Samuel, and the story says that when the witch looked, she reported that she saw spirits ascending out of the earth, and she said that she saw an old man coming "up" out of the depths of the earth, in other words, she was referencing the commonly held concept of Sheol as being deep inside the earth. In the New Testament, Jesus combines elements of Sheol with those of Hades when he teaches the parable of the rich man and the beggar Lazarus:

Luke 16:19 "There was a certain rich man, which was clothed in purple and fine linen, and fared sumptuously every day:

20 And there was a certain beggar named Lazarus, which was laid at his gate, full of sores,

21 And desiring to be fed with the crumbs which fell from the rich man's table: moreover the dogs came and licked his sores.

22 And it came to pass, that **the beggar died, and was carried by the angels into Abraham's bosom: the rich man also died,** and was buried;

23 **And in hell he lift up his eyes, being in torments, and seeth Abraham afar off, and Lazarus in his bosom.**

24 And he cried and said, Father Abraham, have mercy on me, and send Lazarus, that he may dip the tip of his finger in water, and cool my tongue; **for I am tormented in this flame.**

25 But Abraham said, Son, remember that thou in thy lifetime receivedst thy good things, and likewise Lazarus evil things: **but now he is comforted, and thou art tormented.**

26 **And beside all this, between us and you there is a great gulf fixed: so that they which would pass from hence to you cannot; neither can they pass to us, that would come from thence.**

27 Then he said, I pray thee therefore, father, that thou wouldest send him to my father's house:

28 For I have five brethren; that he may testify unto them, **lest they also come into this place of torment.**

29 Abraham saith unto him, They have Moses and the prophets; let them hear them.

30 And he said, Nay, father Abraham: but if one went unto them from the dead, they will repent.

31 And he said unto him, If they hear not Moses and the prophets, neither will they be persuaded, though one rose from the dead."

As I showed earlier, this passage uses the word Hades to describe the location of the rich man after death: καὶ ἐν τῷ ᾅδῃ , "and in Hades." Why would Jesus be mixing the Judaic concept of Sheol with the Greek ideology of Hades? **And when did Sheol start being a place where fire was present?** Just as every Christian today has his or her own personal concept of what Hell must look like, and that view is painted by the brush of every preacher to whom they have sat and listened, people in the days of Jesus all had varying ideas of the afterlife. I, personally, think that Jesus mixed His descriptions using the best local and cultural ideas that would rivet the attention of the listener of that particular time in history and get them to think about life after this existence.

The Valley of Ben-Hinnom

What, then, is geennan? To understand this word, we have to go back to the time before Christ. Solomon had built the largest temple to the pagan god Molech in the valley of the son of Hinnom, or, as it was called in Hebrew, Gei Ben Hinnom. Jeremiah 7:31 says, "They have built the high places of Topheth in the Valley of Ben Hinnom to burn their sons and daughters in

Various illustrations over the years have attempted to depict the image of Molech.

All we know is that this idol was supposed to have the head of a bull, and a great fire was built within it to consume the children that were sacrificed to him.

The mouth was reportedly hinged to open and receive the bodies.

MOLECH.

the fire, something I did not command, nor did it enter my mind."

And, in Psalms 106:36-38, we read: "And they served their idols: which were a snare unto them. Yea, they sacrificed their sons and their daughters unto devils, and shed innocent blood, even the blood of their sons and of their daughters, whom they sacrificed unto the idols of Canaan: and the land was polluted with blood."

Here, in this temple, in this valley, the ancient Jews sacrificed their children in the fires of the god Molech, and for this, the land was later cursed, the temple was torn down, the altars were desecrated, and the best way for "pious" kings to rectify this sin was to defile the entire location by making it a dump for Jerusalem. According to II Kings 23:10, Josiah defiled Topheth as part of his great religious reforms:

"He desecrated Topheth, which was in the Valley of Ben Hinnom, so no one could use it to sacrifice their son or daughter in the fire to Molech."

The valley was used from then on as a perpetual dump for the refuse of the city, complete with burning fires. There are some who argue that there is insufficient extant evidence for this, yet a Rabbi David Kimchi, A.D. 1200, states that this was fact. In Greek, Ben Hinnom, or Ge-Hinnom as it is also called, becomes Gehenna, thus, giving us the word, γέενναν - geennan. Virtually every time the word for Hell is used in the New Testament, the word in the original Greek is Gehenna, the burning fires of the dump just outside the walls of Jerusalem. Since the fires of Molech once burned here, the reference to the fires of Gehenna makes greater sense when preaching to converts who are very familiar with the horrible reputation of this place. This was where the fire and smoke of tormented souls rose seemingly forever.

To the people of the time of Jesus, the Valley of Ben Hinnom, or Gehenna to the Greeks, was full of significantly terrifying history and horrid memories. Here was where the Topheth, "The Burnings," once stood, the very place where the ceremonial drumbeats drowned out the screams of children as their parents sacrificed them into the fires that burned inside of the idol representing Molech. It was here in this same valley that so many ancient kings of Israel had endorsed this horrible pagan practice, even sending their own children into those fires. This atrocious history was common knowledge to the locals. In their day, dead bodies of criminals were thrown there, and anyone visiting there would have seen the worms and maggots eating these decaying bodies among the burning garbage of Jerusalem. Gehenna was a place truly epitomized by the words of Jesus when He referenced it in Mark 9:48 "Where their worm does not die, and the fire is not quenched." What person wanted to think that their body could end up in the unholy and unconsecrated grounds of Gehenna? Yes, the word Jesus used here is Gehenna... not Hell. Just because we say Hell in English instead of Gehenna or Hades, nothing changes. The original Greek text uses Gehenna and Hades, but English translations later changed those words to Hell. So, where does the word Hell come from? Theories abound, but the simple fact is that the modern English word Hell comes from the Old English word Hel or Helle around 725 A.D. and, at that time, referred to the world of the dead in the afterlife, this definition coming from the period of Anglo-Saxon paganism. Prior to that, the origin of this word is steeped in too many theories to nail down, but the word, and its accompanying theology, has certainly evolved over the centuries.

The word Hell has been used in the past, and is still used today, to bridle "sinners" with a fear that is designed to get them to toe a line prescribed by the Church, much like telling children to behave, or the "boogey man" will get them. Sadly, the fear of afterlife torment has been used to keep people in line for centuries in nearly all of the world's religions. Act up, and you are going to pay. One example to ponder is found in ancient Islamic paintings from the 15th Century. In these paintings, the prophet Mohammed is shown visiting Hell. He is riding on his peculiar horse called the Buraq, peculiar because it has the tail of a peacock, but the

15th Century painting depicting the prophet Mohammed visiting Hell. He is riding on his peculiar horse called the Buraq, peculiar because it has the tail of a peacock, but the head of a woman. Mohammed is also accompanied by the angel Gabriel. He is viewing women who are being tortured for eternity while a demon is raking the fires beneath them. Their sin? Going out of their homes without the permission of their husbands.

head of a woman. Talk about male chauvinists. Mohammed is also accompanied by the angel Gabriel. In one of the paintings, he is viewing women who are being tortured for eternity... because they dared to show their hair to strangers. They are strung up by their hair, and a demon is raking the fires beneath them. In another painting, he is portrayed viewing women who are being tortured for eternity. Their sin? Going out of their homes without the permission of their husbands. Research the history of religion, and every religion, every century, every culture, has a list of "sins" that will take your soul to a place of torment after death. These sins vary from culture to culture, from religion to religion, and they vary from century to century. Interestingly enough, **the authors are always <u>men</u>**.

The New Testament passages dealing with Hell and torment are always referencing Greek mythology mixed together when necessary with Judaic elements of Sheol. Notice in Luke 8:31, the writer states that when Jesus cast the demons out of one man, the demons begged Jesus not to send them to "the abyss." Here, the Greek word used for abyss is nothing more than just that, abyss (ἄβυσσον = abusson = abyss). But, it is clear to all by now that this refers to Tartaros. Even in Revelation 9:1-2, 11 and Revelation 20:1-3, the word is the same, abyss.

What we see when we study the origins of the word Hell and its use in the Bible, even parallels in other religions, is that humanity has forever struggled with "The Four Questions Of Life." Who am I? Where did I come from? Why am I here? Where am I going when I leave here? Whether you are Christian, or Atheist, Buddhist or Jewish, Muslim or Bahá'í, you will ALL share one same fact: you will die. And you also share this: since none of us made this universe, and since none of us made ourselves, something greater than ourselves made all that ever has been, all that is, and all that ever shall be. While we as humans struggle with that, it changes nothing in the plans, whatever they may be, of the Creator Force. Just because we strive to figure it all out, even write books like the Bible, the Koran, or the Torah, does not change the Truth, the Truth being whatever it is that the Creator Force has planned. We can guess, but only the Creator Force knows.

One thing becomes apparent the more we study the history behind the various religious texts that are used by various religions to guide their adherents, there have been enough inventions to fill books (as if they haven't already). Each of these books has a varied description of the abode of the dead, the place for the righteous after this life, and the abode for the wicked after this life. They all describe different scenarios. They can't all be right.

The Final Part Of The Four Questions

Read from right to left, the Hebrew words God spoke to Moses, "Ehyeh asher ehyeh," "I am that I am."

From the forces that surrounded me when I was created, I am who I am. When Moses was asked by Pharaoh to tell him the name of who it was that sent him, Moses responded: "Ehyeh asher ehyeh," which is translated roughly as "I am that I am." It could also be "I am that which I am." It all depends on how you want to translate that middle word "asher." But, it is a mysterious way of identifying oneself. What do you mean that you are what you are? And yet, it is an equally metaphysical way of looking at ourselves. I may drive a Mercedes and have servants, but none of those items is "ME." I may be a drunkard dying in the gutter, but that gutter and those clothes are not me. Those bodies, as you will remember, are the "actors" on a stage created by the Creator Force. The real "ME" is residing temporarily within the confines of that body, but that body is going to get left behind. So, too, will the Mercedes and the servants. Who am I? I am a soul who was sent here to this plane of existence, and I was sent here temporarily. This existence is not permanent, so do not fear death. Just as this existence is not permanent, but merely part of a continuum, death is just a doorway.

Where did I come from? I come from the place to which I shall return. I come from a plane of existence not affected by the physics of this plane of existence. Where I came from is the world of reality, and where I am right now is, as the Tibetans teach, the world of illusion. Because it is illusion, who I really am, a soul from beyond here, does not really die. The body ceases to exist when it is time, a time that was preordained before I even came to this plane of existence, but the soul, therein lies the real identity of this body. Remember what I said at the beginning of this book: **I am two beings wrapped together for life, my physical being and my eternal soul. My body is an actor on a stage, and my soul is the true identity of that actor.** I am experiencing this "stage," and it is "coloring" me, just like the forces of pressure take elements from this world and create a diamond and the beautiful colors therein.

I came from beyond here, from beyond this plane of existence. My mother and father were not who actually created me; the Creator Force was. My parents were merely vehicles for my appearance here, the doorway through which I came, but **not** the doorway through which I shall return, for it is from the elements of <u>this</u> plane of existence that the atoms for my body are borrowed and from which I am constructed. My SOUL? That was created elsewhere, and that "elsewhere" is my home beyond this plane of existence. Thus, I came from the Creator Force. **To answer the question of where I am going when I leave here, one only has to understand the true origin of all of us, and that is the Creator Force, and our destiny, therefore, is to return to the Creator Force.**

Why am I here? For the purpose ordained by the Creator Force, to "act" in the "play" that the Creator Force wrote. Part of that design was not to send me here with all of the knowledge of where I come from. When I take a vacation here on Earth, I pack only what I will need for the duration. Use that as your analogy, and you will see that we are "vacationing" here for the experience. If we were moving here to live forever, then we would have brought more with us. **The duration is short in comparison to the eons of existence, but it is of sufficient length for all that is needed for our "experience."**

Thus, we should take this life serious enough to learn, but not to become slaves to it. It is not permanent. When the Bible says to lay up your treasures in Heaven, that is a good way of saying that the purpose of our life is to enjoy our accomplishments, but not become so attached to them that we forget our souls. This is what the theme of the Bible is, after all, the soul "missing the mark," not being prepared for the journey back to the place of the soul's origin. We came here to experience something, but we can get lost in that forest. A movie star becomes so in love with their fame, that they never experience the true joy of helping others. In love with themselves, they grow old and desperately lonely as their once brilliant glory fades into unwanted residue. A millionaire wants zealously to become a billionaire, and loses himself in the agony of never resting for a moment to gain more wealth, alienating all who ever once loved him, and he dies bitter and lonely. The true teachings of all religions, those parts that were threads from the original Truth and not manmade edicts, teach us to be better people, to strive to bring peace to the world around us, to live in harmony, to care for the welfare of those around us. This makes it much more poignant when we read in the Bible, Mark 8:36 *"For what shall it profit a man, if he shall gain the whole world, and lose his own soul?"*

No, you have a purpose for being here. You have a destiny with the doorway of Death. Some call it the "Circle of Life." It is a round-trip ticket. We end back where we came from—home. We came here to go back there. But, we did not come here to sit at the train station. We came here to get on board, to ride that train, to view the scenery, to meet sojourners like ourselves, to enjoy their company, to listen to their experiences, to think and reflect on our own, to marvel at the educational sights, to spend as many days and nights as the trip is booked for. When the train pulls into the station, and we step down from that train, we will find that what we carry is actually in our hearts.

I am a soul within a body that is on a journey in this plane of existence.

I am from another world, I do not come from "here," and I will not stay "here" forever.

I am here to experience what the Creator Force has written.

When this journey is complete, "who I truly am" will return to the place from which "who I truly am" came.

Therein lies the answer to the Four Questions Of Life.

For Your Journey

Do not try to determine the religion of others, but strive to be worthy of your own.

Strive not to be a dictator who forces others against their will to live in a self-made mold, but strive to be a model others wish to follow, because they admire the results your path brings.

Remember that every person is created by God for a reason and with a purpose. Since God does not make mistakes, He has a plan for every life. Be careful of assuming that, when it comes to others, you know what that is.

Knowledge and truth are wonderful things. Love them and pursue them; they will only make you better. But, know what is truth and what is the fear of the universe wrapped in well-rounded, pleasing sayings.

Question whenever and wherever your heart needs an answer. Truth is not changed by questions, but by those who seek not to be questioned.

Avoid the man who says he has the answer to everything. As no man has a monopoly on truth, such a person is a poisonous snake waiting to bite.

Learn to love better. Until you can love everybody, you are not finished. Love does not mean being ignorant of hate, but by being aware of the origins of that weakness, we become more patient and understanding, and, in the process, become guiding lights.

Strive to do something each day for the good of someone else, and let there be no thought of self-reward. Selfishness robs us as a leech placed upon the heart, yet selflessness is like filling the ocean with love.

Finally, understand that you are more than skin and bones and blood. You are an eternal soul destined for somewhere beyond this day. Know that you will take with you all the love and knowledge you possess when you pass through the door of death, yet not one material possession will travel with you.

Remember that, and let your priorities thus be set.

Brian Gray

January 2, 1990

12:57 a.m.

Some final thoughts...

I was raised in a very "religious" household. My father was a Pentecostal preacher of the strictest order. We who grow up as "preacher's kids" know all too well the extra restrictions that come with the territory, and many a preacher's kid has rebelled as they grew old enough to get out of the house. Some, after a bit of time, return to that "ark of safety," a place of comfortable "knowns" rather than face the "unknowns." Guilt, fear, sentimentality and nostalgia all play a role in getting "backsliders" to head home where they are welcomed back with open arms. And that's okay. The climb up the ladder of spiritual and metaphysical knowledge comes with time. The examples of readiness to understand are all around us. I can go through even a small village and take twenty children, send them through school and off to college, and I will have twenty different results. Some will drop out of school. Some will drop out of college. Yet, there will be those who will graduate from the highest level of education with honors. Each person seeks their level of comfort, and each destiny has its rewards.

Religion is the same thing as education. I have seen the good that comes from religion, and I have seen the bad that comes from it, as well. Do we then declare religion worthless? No. Mao Tse Tung made that mistake, declaring it the opiate of the masses and making Atheism the religion of the State. What happened? Mao lies in a mausoleum in Beijing where all can come to view his mummified remains, yet millions in China still seek to console their hearts by worshipping in their various religious ways, some at the risk of being arrested and sent to prison, such is the power of this innate and continuous need within humans. The mistake that Mao made was to assume that all religion is poison, and that everyone can be made into the religious-free image that Mao perceived. No, religion will always play a role in the hearts of humans, because they seek answers to the Four Questions of Life, and this is their way of answering it. However, you should judge any religion and its adherents by what their actions bring.

If your religion brings peace, then it is good. If your religion causes harm to anyone, then it is bad.

If your religion teaches you to love all of God's creatures, then it is good. If your religion teaches you that only "your" kind are good, that all others are outcasts, then your religion is bad.

This is the simple litmus test of any religion. When the Bible says that we are to love our neighbors as we love ourselves, that verse is not followed with a list of exceptions. I have seen too many "religious" people of various religions who do not grasp that valuable teaching. When my religion started to separate me from the people of this world, teaching me that I was better than they were, I left. God made everyone. He made no mistakes. No one is worthless. You can practice whatever religion makes you happy, and I will come worship with you, as long as we are worshipping the One Who Made Us All. When your religion teaches that I am an outcast, that I am unloved by My Creator, I know better. I know who I am, I know where I came from, I know why I am here, and I know where I am going when I leave here. I am spiritual, not religious, and there is a great difference. Religious people follow the dictates of their church, but spiritual people follow the hearts that The Creator gave them. That is the real compass.

On the following pages, I have included three articles which I wrote a number of years ago.

I think they have some relevance to the material contained in this book, so I have included them for your enjoyment.

A photo I took along side of a cornfield after a rainstorm in the summer of 2020.

I'm Leaving It All Behind

    Someone once said, "I've never seen an armored money truck following a hearse." That saying goes well with another one that was made when two people were discussing a wealthy businessman who had passed away, and one asked, "How much did he leave?" Came the reply, "He left it all." Since time began, people have prepared for death in a vast array of manners, and it does not matter what religious beliefs, or lack thereof, they all faced the inevitability of death with one common question—what really awaits? And from that one common question comes a myriad of theories and beliefs. Whether one accepts, by faith, a religious belief, or whether one ties themselves to pure atheism and states that life ends at death, and nothing exists beyond that moment, the actual truth is not changed by either adherence. Examining the burial sites of ancient civilizations and following this examining right up to the present, there are certain commonalities. The deceased had loved ones that had gone on before, and they usually had loved ones who were left behind. The ones who had gone before left some beliefs that were shared with those who were following, and those who were left behind were still somewhat uncertain that what they had been told about death and the hereafter was, indeed, fact. After all, most of what anyone believes about death and the hereafter is based on what we are taught in our societies, in our places of worship, by our loved ones, by what we have read, and finally, by what makes the most sense to us at any given time. Powerfully, what we believe does nothing to change reality, and the reality is this—when we die, and not until that moment, we will finally experience the ultimate truth, the definitive answer of what actually lies beyond this existence.

    Like going over a giant waterfall beyond which we have never been, we can tell each other all the stories we want to as we float down the river of life, stories about the idyll waiting for us beyond that waterfall, but nothing sobers us quicker and makes us ask for greater certainty than the final moment before that great waterfall. Put the question off all you want to, or research it all life long, the answers you accept will mostly be based in faith until that moment of transferring to the "Other Side." I have written before that there are the Four Questions of Life, those being, "Who am I?" - "Where did I come from? - "Why am I here?" - "Where am I going when I leave here?" I, personally, think that the answer to why we are here will only be answered if there is a life beyond this one, a life wherein we are taught that answer. Studying the world's religions, one encounters so many teachings as to what goes on in the afterlife. In the Tibetan view of the afterlife, there is the belief that all life is on a wheel of reincarnation, and when a person dies, that person will either return to this plane of existence, or stay in the afterworld and progress upward from there. In their view of the afterlife, one progresses from one incarnation to the next until that soul, or energy, is reunited and merges with God. If a person is not spiritually prepared at death, then rather than staying in the afterlife, that person will be reborn here on Earth, and the wheel of life continues with another reincarnation. Belief in reincarnation dates to the beginning of history, so it is nothing new, and there are many fascinating books on the subject, such as <u>The Case for Reincarnation</u> by Joe Fisher. Belief in reincarnation is even mentioned in the Christian Bible. As an example, in one passage, Mark 8:27-28, Jesus asks His disciples who the people say that He is, and the reply is that the people think that Jesus might be John the Baptist, Elijah or some other major prophet. Now, how can Jesus be any other person than who He is? This passage points to the acceptance of a belief in reincarnation by the people of that time and place. In another passage, John 9:2, the disciples of Jesus ask Him, "Rabbi, who sinned, this man or his parents, that he was born blind?" Now, look at the question and read it carefully. What these disciples were repeating was commonly held belief in their time and place, that being, reincarnation, and this question is one based in that belief system, since it details the reincarnation doctrine that we pay in our next life for the uncorrected errors in this one. Thus, their question essentially is asking Jesus, who is paying the "karma debt?" They are asking if this man was born blind because of his sins. What sins? He wasn't born, then committed some kind of sin, then was struck blind. Keep in mind that this man was born blind. Therefore, in keeping with the teachings of reincarnation, in order to be born blind as a debt to some sin, he would have had to have committed the sins before he was born. Some Christians get upset with me when I say this, because they think such a statement flies in the face of modern Christian teachings of the afterlife, but it does not. What is related in these two passages is simply a matter of historical fact, that being that many people living in the time and place inhabited by Jesus held beliefs based in reincarnation, and the Bible is merely repeating an example of their reactions to life based in their beliefs system at that time. I am not here to argue for or against reincarnation, merely to show that there are many views as to what happens when we leave our physical bodies for the last time. So, what DOES happen when we die?

If the laws of physics applied, then the one physics law that comes to mind is this: Nothing can be created nor destroyed. Humans do not have the ability to create or destroy anything. Some will say, "Well, if I burn a piece of paper, I have destroyed it." No, you have merely caused a reaction, and the molecules of the paper are now separated into their molecular components, so that, even though they are now in a changed state, the same amount of atoms that were present in the piece of paper are still in the universe. You have not created nor destroyed anything. You have merely rearranged atoms. Using that same logic, if the laws of physics applied beyond life, then what animates your body is energy, the soul, call it what you will, but that animating "entity" separates from the inanimate "body" at death and goes on to its next place in "existence." For the basic Christian concept, the body dies, the soul goes to Heaven. Simple. Easy to comprehend. To the Atheist, there is no God, no Heaven, and in most cases, the belief that the identity of the person ceases to exist at death. Simply put, it is completely over, like a flower that grew, bloomed, faded and died, we simply cease to exist, and the vehicle we used in this life, the body, decays and returns to dust. Somewhat fatalistic and finite. Equally easy to comprehend. After all, both beliefs are based in the same thing, faith. For me, and I have written about this in another of my articles, Does God Exist?, life does not stop at the moment of bodily death. Your physical eyes may close at that moment, but I believe that you will notice absolutely no sensation of time being interrupted. Having been out of my body and into the next realm, even having had interaction with deceased family and friends while there, I am convinced that our existence as "souls" continues uninterrupted. Debate that as you will, but my experience has given me a perspective that is actually not new, since I am not the first person to have an out-of-body experience, and that type of experience has been the source of many writings going back to ancient times. Because there is a vast library of these out-of-body experiences that have been recorded over the centuries, even great discussions, as in the book, <u>Life After Life</u> by Raymond Moody, such metaphysical accounts have been the root of modification of many beliefs systems. Thus, my experience, like so many others who have had the same, has influenced religions down through the ages, and this being mixed in with various religions has produced a colorful tapestry of beliefs regarding the afterlife. Knowing what I personally know, there are still many questions.

I reiterate, nothing will cause a person to want to know the "answers" like the wakening, cold-water splash of impending death. Put it off, exploring the answer, create self-serving theories and mind-salving philosophies, but they will all fail you at the moment when you see Death staring in the window. Then, at that very moment, you may grasp at air, but at that exact moment, your boat in the river of life will have reached the end of the journey, and you will know that it is the end, resigning yourself in whatever emotion best serves you. What is beyond the waterfall now looms, and nothing can be put off any longer. This is where "What-Is-In-Control" shows all of us that we are not "What-Is-In-Control." This is the moment where all the control we thought we had becomes ironic and laughable. Like the scene in the play Our Town, we may have the opportunity to say good-bye, to glance backward for a moment, but, at the moment of death, we are on a moving sidewalk that does not require our legs to move us forward to our destiny. We are delivered to the destination without so much as lifting a finger. Postponing the study of death and dying does not postpone anything but our facing reality. Studying ancient emperors, we find examples of the court magicians tasked with finding the elixir of life, the pills of immortality, the fountain of youth. The emperors thought themselves to be all-powerful, and certainly their power could demand that death be ruled by the powerful. We find so many cases where the magic formula was supposed to make the taker of the formula immortal, and, instead, hastened their death. Laughable in this day and age, since we know that there is nothing that can make us live forever. Live longer? Yes. Forever? No. So, turn away, don't look, refuse to allow the word "death" to be spoken. But, how silly to ignore the clock on the wall of life, when what it should do is be a friendly reminder that we are here for a purpose other than our own personal greed or desire. And, the clock is ticking. Be mindful of it. Our time here is limited. If you need a reminder, take a walk through any cemetery. Beneath those hallowed grounds lie reminders of lives that, just like yours, meant something. They were born, they were nurtured, they grew, they lived, breathed and loved, and when their clock said it was finished, the part that animated those bodies went on to another plane of existence. What then? Only "What-Is-In-Control" knows... but here are some thoughts.

The view of the afterlife has evolved constantly over the centuries. The view that was held by people at the time of Christ was not the same view as was held in the time of Moses. And the Judeo-Christian view most people have today is not at all the same that existed in the time of Christ. Our views and beliefs have changed virtually every generation. Why? For one, we have been exposed to much more science, more medical studies with greater research and more educated minds. These influences have added to the discussion, even though none of this will ever settle the question of the afterlife with a definitive answer that can be accepted as immutable fact. Even in this time in the history of humanity, the answer to that question is still faith-based. However, if there is any credence to my belief that our souls continue to exist, and there is much documentation to suggest that, then the mere fact that they continue on suggests the next thought, and that is, souls are here for a reason, a purpose, and that reason, or purpose, goes with the soul after death. The best analogy I can give is school. We are born, and when we are old enough, we begin an education that is based on levels, or grades. At the end of that education period, we graduate with a degree. Is the "purpose" for the existence of our soul on Earth meant to be an education? If so, what "diploma" do we take with us at the end of it all? Think long on that word "diploma." It most definitely is NOT money! Remember what I said at the beginning of this, how much did he leave? He left it all. Obviously, we do not take our physical possessions with us. Since we cannot take the physical with us as our "diploma," what, then, DO we take? We take the non-physical. We take with us... the "non-physical!"

In my experience on the "other side," I found that we take with us these non-physical things: emotion, ability for communication, identity and all of our memories. I remember when I was out of my body, and I saw my grandmother, my aunt, and two other friends, all of them deceased, I experienced love for them, joy at seeing them, I communicated with them, and I experienced the memory of who they had been while they existed on Earth. This experience, similarly shared by countless others over the centuries, informs my system of beliefs. Thus, for me, there is no waterfall at the end of this "river of life" that my boat is floating on, but rather, there is a dock where I tie off the boat and step out to a welcoming experience in a better place than exists here. What else does this do for me? It tells me that many who live on Earth will miss their "purpose" for being here, that they will have gotten caught up in their material pursuits, squandering the priceless time on that clock, and will have never taken the time to find out why they were really here in the first place. They will "leave it all" behind when they die, all, that is, except for the non-physical elements of the soul. The soul has an identity created by a "Greater Force," and that identity has been modified during life so that it takes that complete identity with it at death. This is why souls immediately recognize each other when they arrive on the other side of life. And because they have memory, they remember one another for who they were in the life before death.

   I remember reading a book many years ago titled, <u>Seth Speaks</u>, in which the author claimed to be channeling the spirit of a man who lived at the time of Christ, the spirit being named Seth, and whether one believes the premise of the book, or simply thinks that the author was delusional, one thing I remember from the book's account was a question posed to Seth and his answer. He said that immediately after death, the soul goes to a place where other souls are waiting to discuss their interactions with that person in the life they just left. As an example, if you had murdered someone, when you died, you went immediately to this "Plane of Reconciliation," as Seth called it, and you met with the person you had murdered. There, you worked out how to come to some resolution on how you had cut short the destiny of the person you had murdered. Of course, anyone who studies ancient religions will see that this idea, or belief, is not new. In the movie, "My Life," the main character, played by Michael Keaton, is a man who is dying from cancer, and life has left him extremely bitter. In one scene near the end of the movie, an Asian doctor is talking with him. The doctor obviously believes in reincarnation and tells him, "You must get rid of all this hate and bitterness. All that you are at the very moment you die is the seed for your next life." Ponderous words. Are our actions actually going to have an impact on our life beyond this one? If you follow the teachings of modern Christianity, you believe that the answer is completely explained in great detail, and that is, your actions here do indeed determine the afterlife situation. Even for those who believe in reincarnation, how you live here on Earth determines a great deal of how you live in the afterlife. And if you are Atheist, then the afterlife may or may not exist, depending on which sect of Atheism you follow. However, even as an Atheist, if all you believe in is the here and now, there is a case to be made for the belief that you will live better in this plane of existence, if you believe that there is a purpose for being here. When you elevate your existence from simply being an evolution of atoms forming into something that is finite and worthless beyond this plane of existence to being something of value in the chain of events that began with the creation of this world, suddenly, your life makes sense. One thing is obvious regardless of your belief system—there have been a lot of humans that have come before you, they all had many of the very same experiences that you are enjoying... and they are all buried. If there is a stone to mark where they are buried, and if there is some bit of memory etched on those burial stones, those stones give silent testimony to life and death, to purpose found, or purpose ignored, to people who knew about the clock on the wall and were accepting, and to people who intentionally disregarded the clock on the wall and tried to fool themselves into believing that it did not matter. I like this analogy. There are two basic types of students—those who get it, study to the best of their ability, and eventually graduate into a useful life filled with making the best of their education; and there are those who thought the entire time they were in school was a waste of their time, dropped out of school and had a struggle all their lives supporting themselves. The former believed in purpose, the latter did not, and the end result becomes obvious at payday.

J. P. Morgan thought that making more money than anyone else in the world, thus becoming the wealthiest person of his time, would gain him the admiration and friends he craved. At his peak, J.P. Morgan paid Carnegie over four-hundred million dollars in cash to own Carnegie's industry. Imagine what that equals to in today's money... billions! Who do you know today who could pull off that monetary feat? No one. Still, like any other human being, he faced life as vulnerable as all other mortals, suffering the loss of his first wife just months after they married and being plagued with rhinophyma which disfigured his nose horribly, forcing him to have all of his portraits retouched. His extreme wealth left him with mental conflicts that ruled him his entire life, and when he died, Morgan was sadly reduced to a mental state of near childlike dependence, bitter at the world, and lonely. His all-consuming passion for making more money than anyone else had created an emptiness that could never be filled, fueling, instead, an ever-growing gulf between Morgan and the everyday people he so wanted as friends. At the extreme opposite end of the spectrum, Mother Theresa gave up the wealth of her family, and found everyone was drawn to her. Mother Theresa will be remembered for the good she did for others while she was in this world. J.P. Morgan is only remembered by financiers who want to see if they can surpass him, having themselves caught the same disease. Am I saying that the deaths of kings and emperors are not mourned? No. Destiny is destiny. For whatever reason a person is born to serve in the capacity of a ruler, or to be extremely wealthy, such a destiny goes back to the four questions of life, and some are born to that purpose. But, emperor or pauper, the inescapable destiny of "end" is the same. J.P. Morgan, with all of his immense power and wealth, could not buy a single day more of life. Different times on the clock, but all finish when their relevant clock hands strike midnight. So, does it matter how you live? How you treat others? What you do for others? What you leave behind? I believe it does. Here's why.

Watching the television docudrama about Bernard Madoff, the famous Wall Street phenomenon who eventually went to prison when his fifty-billion-dollar Ponzi scheme fell apart, I saw the greed for more and more money from those who could never have enough. People invested millions with Madoff, some invested billions, and all of them wanted to make more and more money without really having to do work for their wealth. They wanted to sit back and let Madoff turn their money into more money, and more money, and more money. Millions of dollars was not enough for any of these wealthy investors, and why? What could they not already buy for themselves? How many pairs of pants can one person wear at a time? How many steaks can one person eat at a meal? I am over-simplifying for a reason. What has happened in so many of these lives is that the person involved lost sight of the clock on the wall and felt that they were going to live forever, and that all they had to live for was more and more money. Some will erroneously misquote the Bible and say "money is the root of all evil," but the Bible does not say that. What it does say is that the **"love of money"** is the root of all evil. When you love money more than purpose, you are lost.

A writer was traveling through India to visit the Dalai Lama who has His exile government in Dharmsala. Anyone traveling through India is immediately struck by the virtually indescribable poverty of the majority of its citizens. Yet, while looking out the window of his train as they passed through the countryside on their way north, the writer could not help but notice the many poor people who were smiling and even laughing. Puzzled by this seeming contradiction of life, the writer asked the Dalai Lama how this was possible, that people who seemed to have absolutely nothing of material value could find anything to smile or laugh about. The Dalai Lama's answer was simple, "Their daily needs are met."

My father once gave a parable during one of his sermons. He told of a wealthy man who owned some land above a nearby village that was down in a valley. A spring on his land fed the lake that he owned, and the water from that lake spilled over to form a stream that watered the valley below. Everywhere anyone looked, that land was fertile and green. The crops in the valley were abundant and very healthy, and everyone knew that the water was the source of this abundance. One day, the man stood at the top of the hill and looked down into the valley below. He said to himself, "This is water from my spring that brings all this abundance. It is MY water, and since it is so valuable, I should keep it all to myself. Why should they get it for free?" So, he dammed the lake, and the water was reduced to a trickle. Eventually, the crops in the valley failed. Worse yet, the lake became stagnant and polluted, causing the fish to die, and the rot and stench was more than the man could bear. He tore down the dam and released the water to flow again as it had always been before. With time, the crops returned, the abundance returned, and the joy of this land was restored. The moral of the story was obvious about wealth that is shared, but it also brings to mind the benefits to the soul that come from sharing what we have with others, not giving everything away, but sharing the surplus. Milarepa, the great Tibetan mystic once said, "As long as one desire caresses the heart, the soul will return to this plane of existence."

In Lake Wales, Florida, there is a virtual Garden of Eden called Bok Tower Gardens. With a beautiful bell tower, reflection pool and bird sanctuary surrounded by lush native plants of Florida, one can bask in the solitude and constant quietness of this meditative garden. The land was donated by Edward W. Bok, editor of the Ladies Home Journal, in 1929, and his tomb is there. On it, there are these words inscribed: "Make the world a bit more beautiful and better place because you have been on it." Edward Bok came and went. At some point in his life, he saw the clock on the wall, and he thought about his "purpose" for being in this plane of existence. He nurtured his soul by tending to the souls around him. He left here with memories, he left here with an identity... and the material things? He left them all behind.

Make this world a better place for your having been here.

Bok Tower Gardens—Lake Wales, Florida

If You Had One Year Left To Live...

Imagine if someone were told that they could select any store at their local shopping mall, that they would be given one hour to go through that store, and that they could keep everything that they touched during that one hour. They would be given precisely one hour, no extensions, but everything they touched during that one-hour time limit was theirs for the keeping. Sounds exciting, doesn't it? I can imagine that there are some people who would run to their favorite jewelry store and make a huge pile of exquisite baubles, beautiful pieces that had always fascinated them. Others might run to their favorite clothing store and pick out all the stylish clothes that they had ever wanted, but couldn't afford to buy. The list of stores and the different items people would select would most certainly vary from person to person, because we all do have our personal wants and needs, but the overall idea would be the same - a person given a limited amount of time to make the most of a great opportunity... and that is just like life. Only difference is, we really never know the exact time limit on our own lives.

Like that journey into that store with that one-hour time limit, if you knew that you had one year left to live, what would you do? What would change? Imagine waking up one day, and you discover a pain that wasn't there before. You visit the doctor only to find that you have an incurable illness that will take your life within one year. Your days are now defined by this seemingly unfair constraint. What you thought was some distant day in the far away future, a day that you conveniently ignored whenever it tried to get your attention, now looms before you like a huge, dark cloud. "It only happens to other people," was the subliminal message that always ran through your mind when you read about this person, or that person, who had suddenly succumbed to some dread disease. "Wow!", you said to yourself when reading of their passing, "they were so young." And then you simply went on living your life the way the vast majority of people live their daily lives... as if they are going to live forever.

But, if you knew without any uncertainty that you were going to breathe your last breath on a day that was exactly 365 days from today, what would you do? Yes, there are those who would suddenly say, "Well, that's not fair! Why me?! Everybody else gets to live longer than I do. It's not fair!" You might wallow in depressing thoughts, lots of "woe is me" tantrums, yet none of this would change the timetable. In one year, the life that you have known in this plane of existence would come to an end. Finished. Every future plan that you had entertained? Unattainable. What, then, would be the purpose in continuing to live? You might even bitterly and foolishly consider suicide. After all, if you only have one more year to live, then why live at all, right? Of course, that would just be robbing yourself of the last minutes in the store you selected.

After you have had time to process the fact of your "event" to come, no doubt there would be thoughts about all the time in your past, the good and the bad, of course, but most of all, there would be thoughts about the "What ifs?" When you had finished all of this sorting through the "should haves" and the "would haves," there might finally come a moment of thought that awakens another question - "What now?" You would finally be made acutely aware of the finality of this existence, and a new list would emerge. On that list would be two columns, "Important" and "Unimportant."

Think long about those two columns. Grudges? Animosities? Hatreds? What about all the time spent in front of the television? Video games? Getting drunk? Getting stoned? What about all the things that have rendered you "checked out" while life moves inevitably toward that final moment in the store you were racing through? In one of my favorite movies, "Ghost," the character played by Patrick Swayze turns back to speak to his wife, just as his spirit is about to enter the world beyond this one, and he says something that I find completely compatible with the best Theology. With an amazed and rapturous smile, as if he just discovered the meaning of life, he says, "Love! It's the one thing you take with you!"

This life is not the destination. It is the journey. The destination will come just as surely as the end of a train ride will bring us to the station marked on our ticket. And when we rise to get off that train at our final destination on Earth, even then, another journey will begin. Nevertheless, for now, we are on a fantastic journey through life, a journey filled with wonder and awe, laughter and joy, beauty and love, and, yes, even sorrow and tears. Perhaps we should examine why some of our priorities have imposed limitations on our joys. Even more perhaps, we should examine how we can make the best of the time that we have in this life. And maybe we should see this life as the example I posed early on, a gift from someone who said that we can choose the store of our heart's desire and enjoy it for one full hour collecting everything we wanted.

Brian Gray

November 20, 2016

J.P. Morgan, American Financier

The legendary J.P. Morgan amassed great wealth, yet died lonely and bitter.

Self-Righteousness Stinks

I remember watching the hilarious video of Ray Stevens titled "The Mississippi Squirrel Revival," and one of the poignantly funny pieces of this video came as the video panned to the name of the church over the archway, whereupon we read the words - "First Self-Righteous Church." What follows is a comedic send up of a holier-than-thou-art bunch of "stiff necks" getting into "revival" mode when an errant squirrel gets set loose under the pews. If you want a good laugh, search the internet for the video. It's still up and running, and I still get a laugh when I watch Ray Stevens in his mischievous antics. But one thing about that video always causes me to pause and sort of say an "Amen" as I watch... the words "Self Righteous Church."

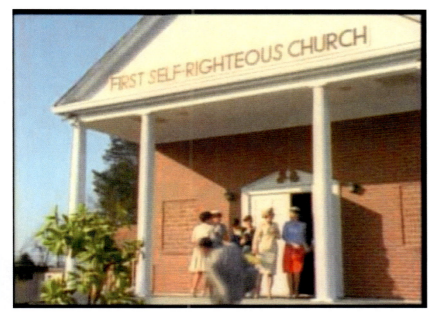

There is not one single sect of Christianity, Judaism, Islam, Buddhism and all the rest, that does not have adherents who tend to get religiously smug. But, since I am a Christian, I am just going to focus on us, we Christians. All religions claim to be "the only Way," and, someday, maybe they can all come together to discuss the problems that come with that exclusionary mindset and how it divides perfectly good human beings from one another... someday. I am not going there in this one. What I am going after are the public figures who wrap themselves in Jesus, God and the Bible, all while acting like they speak for God, and God backs their prejudices and bigotries. And if you think by bigotries I mean homophobes, racists and xenophobes, yes, I will get to them, but I am more concerned with those who are as starched as the Pharisees of old who were so "pure" and "righteous," that there were members of their society with whom they not only could not and would not associate, but with whom they actually refused to be touched by or spoken to, as such would render the Pharisee "unclean."

I see politicians and televangelists acting like these very same Pharisees, perfectly coiffed hairdos, immaculate suits, fake humility and even more fake "holy" speaking manners, as they cluck their tongues, wag their heads in fake dismay and self-righteous shock, and list the horrible things that they see wrong with everyone and everything else... everyone, that is, who does not become a carbon copy of them. And while they look down their noses at the "unclean," they pontificate about why God backs their bigotries and absurd prejudices. I have mentioned in another article about the time I was sitting in church, and the preacher screwed up his face with repugnance and said the following: "Rock and roll music will take your soul straight to Hell." Then, unscrewing his face, he went into "benign mode," as a nearly angelic expression came across his face, and he said, "But country music, now, that's God's music." Really?! We now know what God listens to? This is just ONE example of how Christians allow themselves to be spoon fed bigotry and prejudice, all in the name of God and Jesus, when neither of these two is the author of any of this. And because it comes from the pulpit, we create this false illusion that it thus comes from God, when we should really be remembering that it is a fellow human being, complete with all of the same warts as the rest of us, who stands there behind that pulpit. We should remind ourselves that this person is a product of his upbringing, of his environment, and most importantly, his theological training (or lack thereof). Sadly, we have a religion that is based on a collection of writings called the Bible, but to understand the Bible properly, much training is absolutely necessary... and the vast majority of preachers are woefully under-trained when it comes to such a

A cold, self-righteous prig who goes regularly to church may be far nearer to Hell than a prostitute.

— C. S. Lewis —

The greatest enemy to human souls is the self-righteous spirit which makes men look to themselves for salvation.

(Charles Spurgeon)

powerfully important challenge. But, one thing should be abundantly clear, it doesn't have to be that difficult. God is written in our hearts and souls, He exists in our very DNA, and even if we did not have the Bible properly translated for us, if we looked at the words of Jesus when He recited the two most important commandments, one was to love God with all of our hearts and souls, and the second was to love our neighbors as we love ourselves, we would then see that true Theology does not allow us to judge others, nor does it allow us to show bigotry and hate of any type. Why? Because we don't direct this same harsh acid-bath against our own selves. Why does this second part, to love our neighbors as we love ourselves, get lost in this large community we call Christianity? How does anyone get so self-righteous that they thereupon determine that they have gained an edict from On High to select various passengers to throw off the ark? Who built the boat? Who created the passengers? Yet the self-righteous begin to think that they are both builder and captain.

Can we be "religious" and wicked at the same time? Absolutely! In Isaiah 64:6, we read the words of the prophet as he pleads with God and discusses how Israel has become self-righteous, filled with all of its phony, man-made observations of religious tidbits that had nothing to do with actual spirituality and genuine love of God.

"But we are all like an unclean thing, and all our righteousnesses are like filthy rags; We all fade as a leaf, and our iniquities, like the wind, have taken us away."

Does Isaiah mean that we can never achieve righteousness? No, but what he is saying is that you can be lost in your own religious conceits, so much so that you can become self-righteous and completely miss the mark. This is vital to understand, because I see so many politicians and televangelists who put on airs of righteousness, therefore, they expect no one to be able to speak against whatever bigotry or prejudice comes out of their mouths. They like to wrap themselves in their fake piety, and few there are who will call them on this. Instead, it works like a charm. Who would dare challenge their piety, their sacredness, why, the very rightness of everything they therefore say? And the mindless minions go right along doing their bidding. I find this just as repugnant as the methodology that Hitler used to demonize innocent Jews and turn an entire nation against fellow human beings. Hitler pointed to, and extolled, his genetic superiority, and people bought it. Why? Because it came from higher up than their own lives, their own lives being the commoner and Hitler's level being "the pulpit." It is easy to think that what comes down from "higher up" has to be correct, especially when we fail to examine it against what is spiritually correct. However, what is spiritually correct is what is written in our hearts and souls... and any inhumanity to other humans is always, always, WRONG! Funny how Jesus' teaching of loving our neighbors as we love ourselves gets lost once we start wearing those self-righteous sunglasses.

On a daily basis, I encounter smug, self-righteous Christian zealots who think that their religiosity is what Jesus had in mind when He taught about the righteous inheriting Heaven. But in Galatians 3:11, we read:

"Now it is evident that no one is justified before God by the law, for the righteous shall live by faith."

Further, in Galatians 2:16 we read this admonishment:

"Yet we know that a person is not justified by works of the law, but through faith in Jesus Christ, so we also have believed in Christ Jesus, in order to be justified by faith in Christ and not by works of the law, because by works of the law no one will be justified."

This flies in the face of those who think that their religious strictness in clothing choices, hairdos, even what type of vehicle they use for transportation, such as buggies versus cars, all creates a private and exclusive club of people who are going to Heaven, which they conveniently inhabit, while the rest of us are all left behind, thrown off the exclusive ark, because of our filthiness. We are, of course, filthy and unworthy, simply because we do not adhere to their religious doctrines, and here is the kicker... they cannot have an honest discussion with you about where their "doctrines" come from. They "think" that they know where their religious beliefs come from, but in the majority of cases, they use a standard cop out with, "Well, we believe in the Bible, and the Bible tells us these things." Really? So millions of others who read and interpret the Bible differently are all wrong? And another innocent person is pitched off the ark.

I have lost count of how many people I have talked with who are former members of various sects of Christianity. They all have one thing in common, they had questions that were not being answered, the internal conflicts of what they were taught when it seemed to run counter to what was written in their hearts and souls, and they had problems observing the strict rituals ordered by their "teachers" when these rituals did not make sense either morally or just logically. As one young man who is former Amish told me when I asked him why he left the Amish order, "Too many man-made rules!" Some people can think for themselves, and some people begin to understand that God is in our hearts and souls, that it does not take ritual to commune with God, or even to comprehend the simplicity of the words of Jesus when He told us to love one another as we love ourselves. Is there a place for religious ritual? Absolutely. Many rituals lead us into contemplation of our faith and of our search for a closer walk with God, but when those rituals are required for permission to approach God, and when they become a substitute for actual spirituality and begin to make us think that we are superior to those who do not observe these rituals, we can become self-righteous. Self-righteousness stinks. Everyone can see it except the person wearing it. And the self-righteous person has become so blinded by his need to add badges of religious accomplishment to his puffed out chest that he becomes blind to just how unspiritual he really is.

Thus, when I hear anyone denigrating a fellow human being, because that person is a different skin color, a different ethnicity, a different religion, a different sexual orientation, or any of the other "differents," I choose to follow my heart and soul, the place where I know that my Creator wrote a special knowledge of loving Him and loving His children whom He created. They must be special, if He took all that time and effort to make them. Clever people will always be among us to tell us who we can hate, and they can preach it from their pulpits and congressional platforms, they will even tell us the Bible gives us permission to engage in these bigotries. After all, they are members of the "First Self Righteous Church." Trust them. They built the ark.

Brian Gray

February 22, 2017

Made in the USA
Monee, IL
03 November 2020